START YOUR OWN

MEDICAL CLAIMS BILLING SERVICE

Additional titles in **Entrepreneur's Startup Serie**

Start Your Own

Arts and Crafts Business

Automobile Detailing Business

Bar and Club

Bed and Breakfast

Blogging Business

Business on eBay

Car Wash

Child-Care Service

Cleaning Service

Clothing Store and More

Coaching Business

Coin-Operated Laundry

College Planning Consultant Business

Construction and Contracting Business

Consulting Business

Day Spa and More

eBusiness

eLearning or Training Business

Event Planning Business

Executive Recruiting Business

Fashion Accessories Business

Florist Shop and Other Floral Businesses

Food Truck Business

Freelance Writing Business and More

Freight Brokerage Business

Gift Basket Business and More

Grant-Writing Business

Graphic Design Business

Green Business

Hair Salon and Day Spa

Home Inspection Service

Import/Export Business

Information Marketing Busin

Kid-Focused Business

Lawn Care or Landscaping Bu

Mail Order Business

Medical Claims Billing Service

Microbrewery, Distillery, or Cidery

Net Services Business

Nonprofit Organization

Online Coupon or Daily Deal Business

Online Education Business

Personal Concierge Service

Personal Training Business

Pet Business and More

Pet-Sitting Business and More

Photography Business

Public Relations Business

Restaurant and More

Retail Business and More

Self-Publishing Business

Seminar Production Business

Senior Services Business

Specialty Food Businesses

Staffing Service

Transportation Service

Travel Business and More

Tutoring and Test Prep Business

Vending Business

Wedding Consultant Business

Wholesale Distribution Business

Entrepreneur
MAGAZINE'S

STARTUP

START YOUR OWN

MEDICAL CLAIMS BILLING SERVICE

Fourth Edition

YOUR STEP-BY-STEP GUIDE TO SUCCESS

The Staff of Entrepreneur Media, Inc. & Charlene Davis

EP

Entrepreneur
PRESS®

Entrepreneur Press, Publisher
Cover Design: Andrew Welyczko
Production and Composition: Eliot House Productions

This publication is designed to provide accurate and authoritative information in regard to the subject matter covered. It is sold with the understanding that the publisher is not engaged in rendering legal, accounting or other professional services. If legal advice or other expert assistance is required, the services of a competent professional person should be sought.

Library of Congress Cataloging-in-Publication Data
Names: Davis, Charlene, author. | Entrepreneur Press, issuing body.
Title: Start your own medical claims billing service : your step-by-step guide to success / by the Staff of Entrepreneur Media, Inc. and Charlene Davis.
Description: Fourth edition. | Irvine, California : Entrepreneur Press, 2016. | Series: Startup series
Identifiers: LCCN 2016023346| ISBN 978-1-59918-593-4 (paperback) | ISBN 1-59918-593-8 (paperback)
Subjects: LCSH: Medical fees—Data processing—Handbooks, manuals, etc. | Health insurance claims—Data processing—Handbooks, manuals, etc. | New business enterprises—Handbooks, manuals, etc. | Medical offices—Management—Handbooks, manuals, etc. | Medicine—Practice—Finance—Handbooks, manuals, etc. | BISAC: BUSINESS & ECONOMICS / Home-Based Businesses. | BUSINESS & ECONOMICS / Entrepreneurship. | BUSINESS & ECONOMICS / Small Business. | BUSINESS & ECONOMICS / Careers / General.
Classification: LCC R728.5 .A297 2016 | DDC 610.68/1—dc23
LC record available at https://lccn.loc.gov/2016023346

Printed in the United States of America

20 19 18 17 16   10 9 8 7 6 5 4 3 2 1

Contents

Chapter 10
Blowing Your Own Horn 153

Preface

You're holding this book in your hands, on your lap, or on your desk—probably dangerously near a spillable cup of coffee—because you're one of those people who like to live on the edge. You're contemplating starting your own business.

This is one of the most exhilarating things you can do for yourself and your family. It's also one of the scariest.

Owning your own business means you're the boss, the big wheel, the head cheese. You make the rules. You lay down the law. It also means you can't call in sick (especially when you are also the only employee), you can't let somebody else worry about making enough to cover payroll and expenses, and you can't defer that cranky client or intimidating IRS letter to a higher authority. You're it.

We're assuming you've picked up this particular book on starting and running a medical billing business for one or more of the following reasons:

- ▶ You have a background in the medical billing field.
- ▶ You have a medical background of another sort.
- ▶ You've watched every episode of *Grey's Anatomy, Chicago Med, House M.D., or ER* (depending, of course, on your individual taste and age group) and feel that although brain surgery is a little out of your league, it would be glamorous and exciting to have some connection to the world of medicine.
- ▶ You have a background in bookkeeping and believe that billing is billing.
- ▶ You have no background or interest in any of the above but believe medical claims billing is a hot opportunity and are willing to take a chance.

Which did you choose? (Didn't know it was a test, did you?)

Well, you can relax because there is no wrong answer. Any of these responses is entirely correct so long as you realize that *they all involve a lot of learning and a lot of hard work.* They can also involve a heck of a lot of fun, as well as a tremendous amount of personal and professional satisfaction.

Our goal here is to tell you everything you need to know to decide whether medical claims billing is the right business for you and then, assuming it is, to:

- ▶ get your business started successfully;
- ▶ keep your business running successfully; and
- ▶ make friends and influence people. (That's actually part of Chapter 10, which is about advertising and public relations.)

We've attempted to make this book as user-friendly as possible. We've interviewed lots of people out there on the front lines of the industry to find out how the medical billing business really works and what makes it tick. And we've set aside lots of places for them to tell their own stories and give their own hard-won advice and suggestions, sort of a virtual round-table discussion group with you right in the thick of things. (For a listing of these successful business owners, see the Appendix.) We've broken our chapters into manageable sections on every aspect of startup and operations (the running-your-business kind, not the brain-surgery kind). And we've left some space for your creativity to soar.

So sit back—don't spill that coffee!—start reading, and get ready to become a medical billing pro.

Prescription for Success

This chapter explores the burgeoning field of medical billing, or medical claims processing, from passé paper claims to progressive—and profitable—computerized billing.

Think of this chapter as an investigative report—like those TV news magazine shows but without the commercials.

We will explore the phenomenal growth of the medical billing field and the secrets of America's health-care billing industry.

The Doctor's Key

A medical billing service is the doctor's key to getting paid. Despite the fact that the health-care industry is alive and well in America, most doctors and other health-care providers have no idea how to get themselves paid quickly and efficiently, if at all—either by insurers or by patients who are also waiting for that check to arrive in the mail. Private and government-administered insurance companies, HMOs, PPOs, and a host of other mysteriously initialed plans have conspired to make physician reimbursements as elusive as the pot of gold at the end of the rainbow. Doctors, once the lords of the health-care world, are fast becoming the underdogs. Not to worry—the medical billing service is on hand to save the day. A billing expert can dramatically increase the doctor's immediate revenue.

Through the miracle of cyberspace, the biller electronically transmits insurance claims directly to the insurance company, or, in other words, into the company's check-generating computers.

While electronic claims processing is the industry standard, there are still some providers (mostly smaller practices) stuck in the "snail mail" age. And, since paper processing continues to cause thousands of unavoidable paper cuts, it's beneficial for the MIB (that's medical insurance biller, not "Men in Black") to be familiar with filing both electronic and hardcopy claims.

Not a Small World

With legions of providers and an ever-expanding patient pool, the health-care industry is flourishing. The federal actuaries project health spending will continue to grow by 5.8 percent per year through 2024. By then, health-care spending will total $5.43 trillion and account for 19.6 percent of the gross domestic product (GDP). Consider the historical hard numbers. Americans spent around $3.1 *trillion* for health care in 2014 alone, about $9,086 per person. So let there be no doubt: Health care is big business. And, like Jack's legendary beanstalk, its growth shows no signs of slowing. This makes it fertile ground for the medical billing entrepreneur.

As Rod Serling of *The Twilight Zone* might say, we offer for your consideration the following:

America's ranks are swelling. According to the Centers for Disease Control and Prevention and the National Center for Health Statistics, life expectancy is on the upswing while infant mortality is mercifully on the downhill run. End result: more Americans roaming around. And that means more people to request or require health-care services.

This is especially true since more and more of us are finding ourselves in the once-inconceivable category of Older Americans. Baby boomers—members of the generation born between 1946 and 1964—have already started receiving Social Security retirement benefits. The U.S. Census Bureau estimates the 65 and older demographic will grow faster than the total population in every state, and is projected to reach 88.5 million by 2050. Plus the four million babies born every year are adding ranks to the younger generations who will, one day, be first in line for benefits.

fun fact ☺

The U.S. Census Bureau has a U.S. and World Population Clock you can access through the internet (www.census.gov/popclock/). This site updates the resident population daily by tallying births, deaths, and international immigrant arrivals.

So, in plain English, what does all this mean to someone planning to start a medical billing business? Income.

A plethora of older Americans means more health-care dollars spent at the doctor's office. (As more than one retiree is wont to say, "They ought to call it the Rust Age instead of the Golden Age.") From arthritis to arteriosclerosis to prostate problems, cardiac care and cataracts, it all adds up to more and more money spent on health care (currently around $3.1 trillion a year, if you'll recall). Which, in turn, means more and more Medicare and secondary insurance claims to be filed.

▶ What's a Provider?

In the health-care world, a provider is not only a physician but anyone who provides health-care services. Ambulance services, biofeedback technicians, and social workers are included, along with the non-M.D. doctors we call dentists, chiropractors, optometrists, podiatrists, and psychologists. Doctors specializing in everything from pediatrics to geriatrics, neurology to urology, are also, of course, providers. Purveyors of durable medical equipment, such as walkers and wheelchairs, count. So do specialists in hearing aids and prosthetic limbs. And don't forget nursing homes and hospices. They are providers, as are pharmacies.

These not-so-fine distinctions are important to keep in mind because you can consider them all potential clients for your medical billing service.

What Are People Spending?

Type of Service	Annual Amount*	Type of Service	Annual Amount*
Hospital Care	$971.8	Nursing Home Care	$155.6
Physician/Clinical	$603.7	Dental	$113.5
Prescription Drugs	$297.7	Home Health Care	$83.2

*All figures are in billions. Source: Centers for Medicaid and Medicare Services

FIGURE 1–1: **What Are People Spending?**

Bevies of babies also equal health-care dollars. Think ear infections, colic, colds, chronic diaper rash, and all the other ills junior humans are prey to and you will realize that the rash of babies translates to a steady stream of pediatric patients, which, in turn, translates to a steady stream of insurance claims to be filed. See Figure 1–1, for a breakdown of where health-care dollars are being spent.

Preventive Maintenance

Americans in the age range between teething and losing teeth are also big spenders in the health-care arena. Preventive maintenance used to be something you performed on your car or boat. Now it applies to people.

Just about everybody is into health and fitness these days, which means cholesterol tests, blood sugar tests, weekend athlete injury repairs, liposuction, and psychological tune-ups. People weaned on new medical techniques as seen on television are far more apt to see a doctor for a real or perceived health problem than ever before. Which—again—equals more patients, more bills, and more insurance claims to be filed.

The Problem

However—and this is a biggie—the doctor has little hope of receiving any income from all this patient activity if he can't get reimbursement from the insurance companies.

In the pre-computer world, the payment process was protracted but simple. After being treated, the patient gave his insurance form (with his portion completed, you hope) to the doctor's receptionist and walked away, secure in the knowledge that dear Dr. Whosit

tip

Most insurance companies now prefer electronic submissions. However, if you are submitting a paper claim be sure you know that company's requirements. Many companies post their procedures for filing claims on their websites.

would fill out all the boxes, send it in, and sit back and wait to be paid.

Which was exactly what happened. After a period of up to three months or so, the insurance company, having leisurely processed the form, sent a check to Dr. Whosit. The doctor's receptionist entered the check into his accounts receivable and then billed the patient for the balance. And Dr. Whosit waited another month or more for that money to trickle in.

Sometime in the '80s, doctors decided this system was unfair and began insisting that patients pay for services rendered before leaving the office, send in their own insurance claims, and let the insurer reimburse them.

Nice try. The tables turned in 1990 when congressional law made it mandatory for doctors to complete and submit their patients' Medicare forms. Providers' efforts to achieve timely payments had been foiled again. There is, however, a happy ending to this tale—for the doctor wise enough to employ a medical billing service.

Electronic Filing Beats Paper

Processing paper claims leaves more room for human error. Data can be entered incorrectly or illegibly, forms can be mailed to the wrong address or lost in the mail, and they cost more to process by hand compared to electronic claims. Although Marsha S., an MIB from Georgia, does both paper and electronic, she prefers to file electronically. "The insurance companies will use ANY excuse to not pay a claim, and the easiest one is, 'We did not receive the claim in the mail.' Electronic filing does away with that old excuse," she says.

Medicare gives priority to any claims submitted electronically. Claims received online are paid in 10 to 14 days, as opposed to paper claims, which are set on the back burner for at least 29 days. Most other insurers now follow this same tenet—electronic claims before paper. The results can be dramatic.

Consider this example from a medical biller near Chicago: "[Previously, the client] would type out a CMS [claim form] and send it to Illinois Medicare. It would be

stat fact

The number of people enrolled in Medicare has risen to more than 55 million since it was introduced in 1965, with approximately 10,000 people enrolling every day.

▶ Phasing Out Paper

The CMS 1500 form was recently updated to accommodate ICD-10 codes (International Classification of Diseases, 10th revision) and is used by non-institutional healthcare providers (i.e., family doctors) who are seeking reimbursement from Medicare. The paper claim form can only be used by providers who meet certain government requirements and qualify for a waiver from the Administrative Simplification Compliance Act (ASCA) requirement for electronic submission of claims. So what's wrong with paper? In a word, time. According to the CMS, paper claims providers submit to Medicare must be read with optical character recognition (OCR), a scanning technology that allows hard copy data to be read by a computer and converted to a form that can be used as electronic data. In other words, OCR turns paper data into usable electronic data. The wording, columns, and tables your naked eye sees on the CMS 1500 form are printed in ink that is invisible to the OCR equipment, so only the usable fields can be seen and used. You must use the official CMS 1500 forms available from the U.S. Government Printing Office or authorized printer because they print with Flint OCR Red (J6983) ink. If you print the form on your own computer, your run-of-the-mill ink will show up to the OCR equipment, and it will be returned to you for resubmittal. The moral of the story is, if you are eligible to use paper, use the official forms. Lisa S., an MIB from central Florida, makes things easier by using a template. She just fills in the information on the computer and has it printed right on the form. Similar templates can be found online such as the one at www.mdcodewizard.com/CMS1500/. Look for Medicare CMS 1500 completion and coding instructions, as well as the print specifications in Chapter 26 of the Medicare Claims Processing Manual (Pub. 100-04). This manual can be found at www.cms.gov/manuals/downloads/clm104c26.pdf on the CMS website.

weeks before she'd know anything," he says, describing the way one of his clients used to do claims processing. He took over her billing, shot it off to Medicare, and within four days had online confirmation that the claims had been paid.

He explains that a four-day turnaround is a little faster than usual, and that, while the doctor didn't have the check in her hand, Illinois Medicare's tracking software allowed him to show her that her claims had indeed already been processed.

Needless to say, she was impressed.

Electronic billing might seem like magic, and result-wise, it is. But like stage magic, which is all done with smoke and mirrors, there's a method behind it. It's all done with software, which we are going to discuss in great detail throughout this book.

Skimming Along with Superbills

Superbill forms are productive tools that allow physicians to record patient diagnoses, E&M levels, and procedures performed that includes Current Procedural Terminology, otherwise known as the CPT, and International Classification of Diseases, Revision 10, aka ICD-10. (We will talk about these in more detail later.) The traditional superbill is a double sided 8½ x 11-inch paper with information on it. Even with the new ICD-10 electronic coding environment, the superbill is still regularly used. Doctors who are electronic billing–savvy fill out a superbill (aka a charge slip), before the patient leaves the office. The superbill is divided into sections. One portion lists, in dazzling detail, the services and procedures commonly performed by the doctor. Another catalogs the symptoms and diagnoses the doctor usually treats. Each item on the list has a corresponding code number.

The doctor simply checks the box next to the service or procedure he's performed, makes another little tick next to the diagnosis or symptom, and voilà! There is all the information the medical biller needs.

The medical biller takes this streamlined superbill, enters the procedure and diagnosis codes into a claim form, called a CMS 1500, on his computer and then electronically sends it to the insurance company in the same way you might send an email message. The insurer instantly receives the claim. No more delays waiting for mail delivery. No more lost time waiting for the claim to wend its way through knee-deep stacks of other paper claims. And no more painful paper cuts on your tongue from licking envelopes.

This is the Dick-and-Jane version of modern medical billing. There are many permutations, and there can be many complications, which we will delve into later. (If you just can't wait, check out Chapter 3 now.) Really good medical billers learn all sorts of tips and tricks to make their work easier and to make the doctor's business—and therefore their own—more lucrative.

Heidi H., an MIB from Napa, California, says they receive their superbills in a variety of ways, depending on the provider. Some are streamlined superbills; others are on hospital face sheets. "Providers like simplicity and are stuck in their ways," says Heidi. "So, we will use whatever method they prefer and interpret it from there." Her clients typically send their superbills via email or fax, both of which are through HIPAA-compliant software to make the transmission secure.

stat fact

Last year, the U.S. Census Bureau reported that the number of uninsured Americans dropped to 11.9 percent. This indicates a significant decline over the last few years as more people are able to buy their own coverage due to the ACA's (Affordable Care Act) new subsidized sources of insurance, or they have enrolled in Medicaid or Medicare.

Counting Your Coconuts

What can you expect to make as a medical insurance biller? The sky's the limit, depending only on how serious you are and how willing you are to expand. Annual gross revenues for the industry range from $25,000 to $75,000. Some MIBs are happy working part time at home, bringing in enough to supplement the family income. Others have launched thriving, full-time businesses that employ dozens of assistants.

Kim H., a medical biller in rural Virginia, runs her business in conjunction with a full-time career as a high school teacher. "Keep in mind," she says with a soft twang, "that I'm doing this part time, and with our area here being very small and economically disadvantaged, I had to set my limits." Still, she says, the part-time one-woman income she's pulling in is nothing to sneeze at.

Across the country, a San Diego MIB feels that her fledgling full-time business is off to a good start. At the other end of both the spectrum and the state, Walnut Creek, California, one MIB is well into her 13th year in business with a staff of 22, and is quite pleased with her income as well.

However you choose to tailor your business—part time or full time, at home or in an outside office—the income potential is excellent. But almost everyone in this industry is quick to point out that medical billing is not an easy business.

"This is definitely not something that just anybody could do," explains Curt J., an MIB in Illinois. "Between the personal marketing skills and relating to professionals and doctors, and the learning curve on the code side and the computer side, it's been a challenge. [But] I enjoy a challenge."

One MIB in Denver has offered classes for people interested in starting a medical billing service. "Basically, [I taught] coding, terminology, how to deal with insurance companies, all of that stuff," she says. "And it was really an eye-opener to a lot of people. They just had no clue that to do it right and get and maintain clients you have to know what you are talking about."

Her classes experienced a lot of attrition. "I had probably about 50 percent who felt it was too much work," she explains. "They really wanted something where they could just pick up superbills, put them in their computer, and not worry about it again. And that just doesn't work."

stat fact

According to the Census Bureau, there were 5.5 million Americans aged 85-plus tootling around the country at the time of the 2010 census. That represents increases over 2000 census figures of 29.8 percent in the 85- to 89-year-old category; 30.2 percent in the 90-94 category; and 25.9 percent in the 95 and over category.

▶ One for All

The medical biller's most basic tool is the CMS 1500 (formerly the HCFA 1500). This daunting form is a detail-lover's dream, rife with boxes, bars, and spaces to be filled in, checked off, and tabulated, and is used to file all insurance claims. The CMS, as it is commonly referred to (though some still call it the HCFA), is the brainchild of the American Medical Association and is named for the Center for Medicare and Medicaid Services (CMS).

Before 1984, when the original HCFA 1500 was born, hundreds of different claim forms floated across the medical biller's desk: the American Medical Association's basic form and various versions of Medicare, Blue Cross, Blue Shield, Medicaid, and Civilian Health and Medical Program for the Uniformed Services (CHAMPUS) forms. In addition to these, most insurance companies had their own forms. The horrendous hodgepodge of blanks to be filled in was not only time-killing but conducive to error.

The American Medical Association (AMA) decided that enough was enough and created a task force to bring forth order from chaos. The result was the HCFA 1500, a single, standard form accepted by every insurer in the country.

In 1990, the HCFA went under the knife for further streamlining. The spaces where providers could write in explanations for out-of-the-ordinary fees were eliminated, lending the form the same impatient "I don't want to hear any excuses" tone you used to hear from your parents when you were in trouble. Now called the Center for Medicare and Medicaid Services, or CMS, the group is the main governing body for all things governmental as related to health care.

Balance that with the words of an MIB in New Jersey who quit a ten-year career on the other side of the fence—working for a health insurer—to operate her homebased business. "I loved my job," she says. "I loved being on that side. But I would never go back to working for someone else, either."

Crank-Up Costs

One of the catch-22s of being in business for yourself is that you need money to make money—in other words, you need startup funds. These costs are relatively small for a medical billing service. You can start out homebased, which means you don't need to worry about leasing office space. You don't need to purchase a lot of inventory, and you probably won't need employees. Your basic necessities are a computer (it's hard to do electronic filing

► Prognosis: Success

So now that you have a nodding acquaintance with some of the many facets of this vital business (the formal introduction will come later), you're probably wondering what your chances of success are. After all, starting a business is a serious proposition, particularly when you have to put your hard-earned money where your CMS 1500 is.

Well, take heart. There's plenty of life in this business if you're willing and able. Perhaps even more important, you can make a go out of this profession no matter where you live, according to Tammy Harlan, president/CEO of Medical Billing Course, LLC, a medical billing training company in LaPorte, Indiana. "We service 800 clients, and the biggest one is a $2.5 million operation in Nebraska," she says. "When I operated my own medical claims service, I worked out of Indiana, but I had clients as far away as California. Word of mouth helped me get new business, and I was willing to spend the money needed to get the appropriate business resources and training."

We'll talk more about those business resources later. But for now, just remember that your own ambition and motivation are just as important as upfront money when it comes to driving your success. As mentioned earlier, attention to detail and persistence are other necessary components for success in this people-driven field. Plus, there are numerous outside forces that can influence your success. For instance, if you live near a large metropolitan area, you'll have a larger pool of prospects to plumb, plus you'll be able to charge more per claim. Being internet savvy (or being willing to learn) also will help you increase your reach even further.

If you like to eat regularly, you might want to ease into your new profession. Realistically speaking, it could take several months before you land that first client. But whatever you do, Tammy says, you need to invest in all the tools you need to make it work, including business support and instruction.

"I know it's hard to spend money when you're just starting out, but it's an investment," Tammy says. "You might end up spending $8,000 to get started, but you could end up with a business for the rest of your life."

without one), internet connection, a printer, a telephone, a fax machine, reference materials (coding books), and a specialized software package. If you already have a computer, your biggest expense will be your software.

Many MIB newbies opt for a business opportunity package, purchasing not only the software but also the training to go with it. Different packages, even within the same company, have different costs. Some entrepreneurs go with strictly software because they're already billing-literate; for others it's because the full biz op package doesn't fit into their budget.

The choice of which package to purchase is a personal one, approached by most MIBs with the same dedication and attention to personalities as you would attach to finding a mate. And rightly so. You are going to be wedded to your software package for a long time, and the business opportunity vendor you choose should fit your needs and your temperament like Adam and his rib.

We'll cover this in greater depth later in this book. For now, let's say that you can expect your startup costs to run from about $5,000 to $20,000.

The Rock of Gibraltar

In addition to profits and startup costs, two other important aspects to consider are risk and stability. You want a business that, like the Rock of Gibraltar, is here to stay. According to MIBs, there aren't any tremors rocking the structure of the industry. The risk factor is relatively low—so long as you are willing to work, and in most cases work hard, for that first client or two. "Doctors aren't just out there ready and waiting for you to walk through the office and save them," says the Illinois MIB. It can take time.

"Getting that first [client] is the toughest," explains the San Diego entrepreneur. "It's really tough, because if you don't have a client, then you have no basis, no credibility for [doctors] to rely on you. This is a big thing that they're giving up. A lot of doctors have a hard time giving up the financial end of things.

"Some people are looking for a get-rich-quick scheme. This is not the type of business to do that. You can be successful and make good money at this, but like any business, I believe, it takes time for the business to build, and it takes time to generate a positive influx of income."

> **save**
>
> Why not work at home? A medical billing service is a perfect candidate for a homebased business. The necessary equipment fits neatly into a spare room and, since clients don't need to visit your office, you don't have to spend startup dollars on expensive furnishings, décor, or reception areas.

The Right Stuff

OK, so you've decided that running a medical billing service is potentially profitable. You're willing to invest not only the money but the time to learn the ropes and become established as a pro. What else should you consider? Personality.

▶ Traits of the Trade

Hey kids! Take this fun quiz and find out if you have what it takes to become an ace MIB.

1. *My idea of a fun evening is:*

    a. Watching *Casablanca* on television for the 50th time

    b. Snuggling up with a hot toddy and a book of advanced sudoku

    c. Barhopping with a guy named "Swinger Pete"

2. *Here's how I handle my daily mail:*

    a. Pick out the Publishers Clearing House and Overdue! Second Notice! envelopes, and throw the rest in a drawer.

    b. Sort it by date received, date due, and action to be taken.

    c. Use it to start a fire in the barbecue pit for tonight's dinner.

3. *I consider myself to be a detail-oriented person.*

    a. True

4. *There is nothing wrong with Question 3.*

    a. True

    b. False

    c. Sorry, I wasn't paying attention.

5. *I would best describe my self-motivational abilities as follows:*

    a. What is self-motivation?

    b. I'm not happy unless I'm getting things accomplished.

    c. I'm able to get up in the morning.

Answers: If you chose B for each answer (and you noticed that there is no B answer for Question 3), then you passed with flying colors! You have what it takes to become an MIB. You are detail-oriented, self-motivated, and eager to learn.

Not everybody is cut out to be an MIB. This is not, for example, a career for the organizationally challenged. If you're one of those carefree folks who take a haphazard, devil-may-care approach to life, you don't want to be a medical biller. If your idea of filing is throwing papers in a stack behind your desk until the stack topples, you might look elsewhere for job inspiration. If you're an A-plus procrastinator who can't seem to return a phone call or pay a bill until it's overdue, think again about medical billing.

If, on the other hand, you're an efficient time manager, you excel at detail-oriented tasks, and your idea of heaven is getting things shipped out, shaped up, signed, sealed, and delivered, then this is the career for you.

Move Over, Miss Moneypenny

This doesn't mean that only super secretary types like James Bond's Miss Moneypenny need apply. MIBs come from all walks of life. The entrepreneurs interviewed for this book, for instance, come from a variety of careers: high school teacher, former pastor, computer customer service engineer, registered nurse, and bookkeeper. Others made less radical career-style changes, having worked in the health-care, insurance, and medical billing professions before, but as employees rather than as the self-employed. One ambitious MIB launched right into her own medical claims billing service fresh out of school.

The tip here is that the first ones—the set that started from different career paths—have figured out how to make their backgrounds work for them in their new careers. They've taken the skills they've already acquired and applied them to the medical billing service.

For Kim H., the computer and business course teacher from Virginia, picking up electronic billing was a snap. So were the small-business aspects of running a medical billing service, which meant the only thing she needed to focus on was the actual medical coding.

"I knew a lot about the business part of it and the computer part of it," Kim explains, "but the insurance part I didn't know, so I had to learn that. It took me about two months to really grasp the insurance part. The year I started my business, I got [the business opportunity package] in January. By May, I had signed my first doctor, a psychiatrist. I guess about three months after that, I signed a urologist." Kim now has two more clients to keep her busy along with her full-time teaching career.

People Skills

Curt J., a former pastor, transferred his people skills to his medical billing service which he launched over a decade ago. "My personality is such that I can make a fairly good first impression," he says, describing his marketing approach. He had no background in sales, but Curt says that as a pastor, he knew how to get along with people. Part of his pastoral training was in working with people. "It's all personal skills but, in a sense, it's selling, too.

"The learning curve [for medical coding and billing] was much greater than I anticipated. It's not a simple business. I wanted to pick one that looked like it had potential for the future and could make money, but, on the other hand, I didn't want to pick one that just anybody could do," Curt says.

Mary V., the former customer service engineer, translated the people skills she'd learned working for IBM—as well as her knowledge of computers—into the medical billing business she started more than ten years ago. "Basically, as a customer engineer," she says in a lively but no-nonsense tone, "all you did was problem-solve. And that's what this business is—problem solving.

"Learning to work with people, I couldn't have gotten any better training. Personally, I think [IBM] is the best service company in the world, and they have the best training. So that was perfect for going into this. Whether it's medical billing or anything else, if you're dealing with a service-oriented company, you've got to know how to give service. And that's what this is."

Sandra S. from Minnesota got her people skills on the job by working in medical claims for 20 years starting with a major insurance company, then as a subject matter expert with a state insurance company. She now has her own medical claims consulting business that offers services to individuals needing help with filing claims or reviewing their claims for correct payments and submission to multiple insurance providers. "My niche is in research," Sandra says. "I love digging for answers and finding the correct information to get a provider or a patient the information they need to get their issues resolved."

One nurse-turned-MIB received her training in England. "When I came over here," she explains, "I tried to transfer my credits over, but at that point in time it was not possible. I had to go back and do some retraining, and I chose not to do that."

The career path she chose instead led, not quickly, but very directly, to the exact skills she would need to run her own highly successful medical billing business. She became an audiometrist, then a medical assistant at an ear, nose, and throat practice. "And within a year," Jan says, "I was administrator of that group." With more than 11 years of experience at that position, "I went into hematology-oncology and was an administrator for a large practice for six years before starting the billing service."

The other registered nurse spent almost 12 years on the post-op surgical floor. When an on-the-job injury permanently sidelined her career in scrubs, she parlayed her knowledge of the medical field into the medical billing service she now successfully owns and operates.

The former bookkeeper, Carol G., took her familiarity with all things billable and segued it into her own medical billing service. "I've worked for small businesses," she says, "and you work hard. You can only make so much per hour. It's nice to have a little more of what you're working for be on my end instead of working for someone else."

And isn't that one of the main reasons for starting your own business? The freedom to do things your own way, at your own speed, in your own home or office, is a powerful lure.

The Great Debate

As you can see, you don't have to have a medical background to become a top-notch MIB, but it helps. Marsha S. is an MIB lifer, working with medical claims billing for 25 years starting right out of high school. "The last ten years have been in surgery billing, so that is what I am currently most proficient at," she says. "However, I have done everything from dental, to primary-care medical, surgeon billing, pediatric, orthopedic, and ambulatory surgery billing."

Among MIBs, however, a debate of sorts rages. Those with medical billing backgrounds insist that without that background, only fools rush in. Those who came into the business from other venues admit to the challenge of a major learning curve but are proof that with

▶ The Self-Starter

Being a self-employed MIB, like everything else in life, has drawbacks along with the perks. A big one is that you have to be what is commonly referred to in help-wanted ads as a "self-starter." There's no one else around to tell you what to do or when to do it. If you want to run a medical billing service, you'd better make sure that your self-motivation gears are well-oiled.

"Even if I have my clients' billing done," says Carol G. from her home office in Missoula, Montana, "I'm making contacts or I'm looking at ideas, or if I hear of someone, I'm making that advertising contact."

You also need to keep in mind that all the responsibility for your business rests on your shoulders, however broad they may or may not be. "At times, you wish you could sit back and let somebody else fix the problems," the former bookkeeper explains. "The good and the bad stop right here."

But you don't feel bad about it, Carol's quick to add. "Even when I was working full time, when I would come to work [in the medical billing home office], it wasn't work; it was what I was enjoying doing. You have to discipline yourself to make it what you want with those things in mind."

a great deal of preparation and hard work and the added bonus of support from a software or business opportunity vendor, it can be done.

The nurse whose background involves years of medical office administration is of the "no prior experience, no success" school. "It's the Johnny-come-latelies who don't do terribly well," she says sympathetically but firmly. "Maybe some lady who believes in starting a billing service, working on a PC in her home, and has had experience in billing, can probably do very, very well. If it's somebody who believes that it's just an easy thing to do, that person is in for some pretty rude awakenings. A lot of businesses that are in homes are not making it; their experience is not adequate to do what they're doing." The Denver MIB works from her home rather than from offices in a commercial building, as her San Francisco Bay–area counterpart does, but she voices similar sentiments. Like her cross-country compadre, she started her business with an extensive background in medical billing and administration.

aha!

Ask a billing service to let you sit in on their operations for a few days. You can "audit" the service, observing what they do and how they do it. (You might want to pick a service outside your own area so you don't look like a competitor.) Or, why not volunteer to work for them for free for a few weeks? You get free experience and on-the-job training; they get free labor and a chance to strut their stuff.

"I started working in a physician's office as a receptionist," the Denver-based MIB says. "I became office manager, [then] I worked as a personnel trainer in the medical field. So I've always been behind the front desk. I never really did the billing until I moved out here to Denver and worked for a large billing service and got familiar with the insurances they use out here. And [then I] decided that I could do it on my own. I really liked that aspect of it.

"Since I had worked for physicians as a receptionist and a transcriptionist, I felt that I knew what went on in the office and could provide a good service rather than some of the billing services—some of the larger ones, anyway—that aren't really familiar with the inside workings of a physician's office. I felt that helped me a lot in kind of working up from ground zero."

She also thinks that this wealth of experience represents the dividing line between the successful medical billing services and those that face a struggle. "I taught some evening classes on how to bill for a time simply because I had a lot of phone calls," she explains. "People who wanted to [know] 'How did I get started in this business?' 'I'm thinking about doing this from home,' that kind of thing. One of the questions I always asked was 'What kind of experience do you have?' and most of the time what they would say was 'Well, I know computers.'

"And that's the big fallacy. I find it comes from software companies who are selling the billing software: 'We'll train you; you don't need any experience; all you have to do is put the data in.'

"That's just unfair. That's unfair to people to spend money on software and think that they can just enter data. What I say to them at that point is, 'How are you going to speak to a physician and convince him that you can

tip

"If you're really going to succeed in it," Mary V. says of the MIB industry, "you're going to have to [be learning] almost every day." Be sure you're willing to make that commitment.

handle his money and that you can bring in money for him when you don't know what he does and you don't know his medical turf?'"

What exactly do you need to know? Why wouldn't a person be able to pop a diagnosis of X into the computer, and away they go?

"Well, they can enter it into the computer," the Denver MIB cheerfully concedes. But there is more. Much more. "It's not so much the diagnosis—well, it is the diagnosis, just as much as it is the procedure code. Say they have a diagnosis of depression. They put it in with just an office visit and send it out to the health-care company, and the health-care company sends back a denial saying 'We're not going to pay this. This is a mental disorder.'

"What then? Does someone who does not have the knowledge know how to handle that? All of a sudden they're stuck. 'OK, I'm not going to get paid for this; I don't know why.'

"It's the wrong code. It's only going to get paid at 50 percent; they need to send it someplace else. They need to know what a mental disorder code is and when you can and can't bill for it, who can bill for it, whether you bill the health insurance or you bill the mental side of it. They need to know also that the doctor does a visit, but then he does a test, too. You put the visit in, and you put the test in for the same date of service. The insurance company isn't going to pay for the visit unless they have a modifier code on there. Someone who doesn't have the experience with coding or any experience in medicine [isn't] going to know to put that code in to get that money for that doctor."

The Denver MIB suggests that would-be medical billers with no prior experience take a job for a year with a billing service and learn from that. The Minnesota MIB agrees. "I would recommend working for a hospital or a doctor's office for a couple years as a biller/coder before trying to work from home," she advises. "As a new biller you will benefit from working in an office setting to see what works and what does not."

At least attend some one-day seminars on coding or weekend workshops on business management that are held in most cities so you can get a grasp of what kinds of things are going to be expected of you.

Looking back, the Napa MIB who started her business fresh out of medical billing school feels that she would have benefitted from working in a doctor's office a little while. "I had no previous experience in medical billing or working in an office," she says. "On the other hand, working for a billing service might have been better because you learn about billing for different specialties." Although it took Heidi H. almost two years to land her first client, she now has six employees working out of two locations in California and Oregon.

Starting Over

On the other side of the Great Debate fence, Mary V.—the former customer service engineer—explains how she geared up for her business and what sort of training and research she has in her battle chest.

"My background was with IBM. I'd been in that for close to 20 years and got downsized, like 56,000 others," Mary says. "Actually, I started as a customer engineer working on machines, which was unique in itself because women just didn't do that when I started. I was the fourth female hired in the Baltimore/Washington area to do that." By the end of her tenure, her beat was lease billing. "Basically, whenever billing time came around, I was on call, 24 hours a day."

Then came the downsizing. IBM offered its soon-to-be-ex-employees various classes in job placement and interviewing. One was in entrepreneurship. "A friend of mine and I said, 'Well, we've got to waste three days someplace, so let's go,'" recalls Mary.

A couple of programmers in the class had checked into medical billing, Mary remembers. "The more they talked over the three days, I thought, 'These two are the only ones who have a shot at making anything go.' And basically, that was it. I tucked that in the back of my mind. Once I left, I never thought about it again until I was told in a job interview that if I wasn't willing to work six months at a time or a year at a time, that I would never work again. And so I thought, 'Well, thank you very much, I don't want to do this again. I'll try something else.'

"That's when I started thinking about medical billing again. So that's how I got into it initially."

After purchasing her first medical billing software package, Mary says, "As I got deeper and deeper into it, I found I needed to know a heck of a lot of stuff. So I took classes at the community colleges; any seminar that [came] up, I was there. Anywhere that I could get knowledge on this [industry], I would go. And I still go."

Today, Mary has a client base of 14 providers. Not bad when you consider she had no medical background going into the business. You must also consider, however, that she set out to learn whatever she could at the outset.

My Friends, the Doctors

Curt J., the former pastor, began his business with no medical background, either. "Basically, I was playing with my computer at home, wasting a few hours a week. I needed extra income, so I began to research how I could meet the need and work with my computer, which I was having fun doing. So I basically just started looking on the internet for businesses, and I looked at *Entrepreneur* magazine and things like that. I kept boiling it down until finally I arrived at medical billing as the option I wanted to pursue."

After a great deal of research, he went with a business opportunity vendor in Arizona. After flying out for training, he returned home to get his fledgling operation off the ground. "I just started knocking on doors and visiting and sharing materials and so on and so forth," Curt says. "Now, I bill for one dentist and two chiropractors."

Although Curt had no medical background, he had friends in the business. "The reason I got into it," he says, "is a couple of my friends are doctors. One was a dentist, whom I'm billing for. I didn't want to deal with just the general masses and marketing or retail or anything like that. That's part of what appealed to me, too; the clientele are business owners, office managers, and doctors."

But he echoes the sentiments of everyone on both sides of the Great Debate. "In my opinion there's no way you can just buy software and get into this business. I made dozens of phone calls—and still do—back to [the business opportunity]," says Curt. "I can't imagine anybody just buying the software and doing this, unless they have a lot of medical background."

Summing Up

So, like ladies and gentlemen of the jury in a celebrated court case, you've heard both sides of the argument. To sum up, one side stands firm that without a medical background, you're asking for trouble. The other side stands as proof that a background in medicine or medical billing is not a prerequisite for MIB success.

You should note, however, that both sides agree on an important issue: If you don't have a medical background, you must be willing to work hard in your new field. You must take into account a major learning curve.

You can succeed—brilliantly—but you have to be willing to pay the piper.

The Prognosis

If you're still reading, we assume you've decided to take the MIB challenge and forge ahead with your new career. There is, however, one more thing to take into consideration: the industry prognosis. Will medical billing be around as technical advances unfold in the 21st century?

The future looks good. As we saw at the start of the chapter, there's a great big beautiful tomorrow for the health-care industry. Unless a meteor from outer space crashes into Earth, or unless aliens from the planet Zark land on the White House lawn and show us how to eradicate injury and illness for all time, the industry outlook is healthy.

It is possible that a national health-care plan will finally come to pass and the manner in which health-care is billed and paid for could change. Doctors, however, will still have to be paid, and patients will still have to file claims. Somebody will still have to file them, and who better than the MIB?

So, fasten your seat belt, bring your tray table to the upright position, and let's start your learning curve. Next chapter: Health Insurance 101!

Health
Insurance 101

There's much more to medical billing than meets the eye. Even though the CMS 1500 mainstreamed the claim form, the MIB's world is full of corporate and governmental entities whose main goal in life often appears to be obstructing easy claims processing.

As World War II posters frequently reminded: "Know your enemy." Keeping up with changes—an important part of the medical billing industry—is easier when you understand where insurers are going, as well as where they've been.

It's also extremely necessary to speak the lingo, to be able to rattle off information about carriers, administrators, beneficiaries, and comprehensive plans and actually know what you're talking about.

Who's Who in Insurance

The Carrier. This may sound as if it is referring to someone you'd rather not get up close and personal with, like Typhoid Mary, but in fact it refers to the insurance company that writes and administers the insurance policy. The carrier is also known as the *insurer, underwriter*, or *administrator*.

Each carrier can offer a variety of insurance plans. A single carrier might sell individual policies and group policies and administer a federal program such as Medicare. These plans—which can be worded as craftily as a government foreign aid policy—fall into three basic groups:

1. *Individual policies.* These are purchased by (surprise!) individuals rather than by or for groups, although they can cover an individual and spouse, or an individual and family. Homeowners and vehicle insurance policies also provide health-care benefits to cover, for example, an auto accident, a dog bite, or a fall on a frozen front walk.

2. *Group policies.* This is the package deal concept. Most group policies are provided by employers for their employees. In some cases, it's a freebie; in others, the employees pay for the insurance with the idea that their cost is lower than it would be if they purchased the policy on their own. Group policies are also purchased by (surprise!) groups for their members, such as the Romance Writers of America or the Good Sam Club.

3. *Government programs.* Although Medicare, Medicaid (including the Affordable Care Act), the Children's Health Insurance Program (CHIP), and TRICARE (provides civilian health benefits for military personnel, retirees, and dependents) are government entities, they are administered by the private sector insurance companies or data processing firms.

The Provider. This refers to the person who provides health-care services and/or supplies. A provider can be a physician, pharmacist, physical therapist, outside laboratory performing various tests, or a medical supply company that rents or sells wheelchairs or walkers. In the medical office, the doctor is considered the provider even when it is the nurse or assistant who draws the blood or performs the test.

The Beneficiary. This is the person eligible to receive benefits under the health insurance policy—simply, the patient.

The Insured. This is the policy holder, the person who is covered by the insurance program and who makes it possible for his or her family to be covered. In other words, the insured is the employee whose employment makes the group coverage available. The insured can also be referred to as the *enrollee, certificate holder*, or *subscriber*.

The Dependents. These are the children (including stepchild, legally adopted child, or foster child) and spouse—or in some areas the domestic partner—of the insured. Policies define covered dependents using these criteria:

stat fact

Whether you love it or hate it, since the Affordable Care Act went into effect the uninsured rate among U.S. adults declined to 11.9 percent. This has provided more job opportunities for medical insurance billers and coders.

- ▶ *Spouse.* The insured's spouse (or domestic partner, if applicable) must not be legally separated from the insured and must not be in the armed forces.
- ▶ *Child(ren).* The Affordable Care Act now extends coverage for young adult children under their parent's health-care plan up to the age of 26, regardless of their financial dependency, residency with parent, student status, employment, and/or marital status.

Now that we have established who the players are, let's look at who is making the rules. There are more than 1,000 health insurance companies in the United States, with different types of plans. Health insurance coverage falls into several categories including private,

▶ Get with the Group

Group insurance frequently takes the form of a self-insured plan. In this type of program, the employer, rather than an insurance company, provides the funds to pay its employees' claims. Simple, you say. But wait! It then often hires a TPA (third-party administrator) to administer the plan. The TPA can be an insurance company or a specialized management company. Sometimes this employer/administrator arrangement is called an ASO, for administrative services only.

Or, it can take the guise of an MPP, which stands for *minimum premium plan.* In these plans, the employer goes the self-insurance route up to a certain dollar amount and then pays a commercial carrier to take on the risk for everything over and above that sum.

► The Exclusive Exclusion List

When an individual or group buys health insurance, the contract between the purchaser and the carrier spells out the coverage provided, as well as the limitations of that coverage. The more limits there are, the lower the cost to the purchaser. The insurer is obligated to cover (and provide reimbursement for) only those services specified in the contract. Here are some of the general factors that limit this coverage:

► *Listed exclusions.* A policy can list specific services, procedures, and/or supplies as being excluded from coverage; for example, maternity care, dental care, or surgery to implant the Hope Diamond as a permanent wrist ornament. No benefits will be paid for listed exclusions.

► *Pre-existing conditions.* As of January 1, 2014, health insurance companies can no longer refuse to cover benefits or charge more due to a pre-existing condition. The exception to this are "grandfathered" health plans.

► *Maximums.* Most policies will pay specific maximum dollar amounts. These can concern a specific illness or be annual or lifetime maximums.

► *Annual maximum.* If a policy has an annual coverage maximum on elective or non-essential health benefits, it will pay no more than that amount in a benefit year or calendar year, depending on the terms of the policy. Essential health benefits (see Glossary for definition) no longer have a dollar limit under the Affordable Care Act.

► *Lifetime maximum.* The same is true for lifetime limits for which there are no dollar limits the entire time an individual is enrolled under a specific plan. Again, this only applies to essential health benefits, as defined in the Glossary.

► *Mental and addictive disorders.* Insurance policies routinely include separate schedules of benefits for mental, psychoneurotic, and personality disorders, and for the treatment of drug and alcohol addictions. These items might be excluded entirely, or they might be subject to limitations.

► *Deductible.* The amount and type of deductible depend on the policy, with the deductible usually directly related to the premium. The insured may opt for a higher deductible in exchange for a lower premium, or he may go for a plan with no deductible that specifies care from certain providers.

► *Individual/family deductible.* In some policies, each covered family member must meet his or her own deductible. In others, all the family's expenses go toward a single deductible.

► *Co-insurance.* This standard provision requires the insured to share the cost of certain covered services. The insured must pay either a set fee for a given service or a specified percentage of the cost of that service.

employment-based, Medicaid/CHIPS, Medicare, military (i.e., TRICARE), and workers' compensation.

Commercial Carriers

Commercial carriers offer health insurance contracts to individuals and groups. Think the big traditionals— Aetna, Humana, and UnitedHealthcare—for an idea of what we are talking about here. But, of course, there are thousands of smaller carriers as well. As opposed to various altruistic government or nonprofit carriers, commercial carriers are in the health insurance business to make money.

> **fun fact** ☺
>
> The U.S. Census Bureau, self-proclaimed "pre-eminent collector and provider of timely, relevant, and quality data," conducted its first survey in 1790. On the medical timeline, this was just six years before Dr. Edward Jenner developed the smallpox vaccine.

Some commercial plans are *indemnity* policies. This does not refer to the classic Fred MacMurray film about murder to collect life insurance but rather to the fact that the carrier *indemnifies*, or reimburses, the patient for covered services up to a limit set in the policy. For example, it might pay for mental health services up to a yearly limit of $1,000 or a lifetime limit or cap of $10,000. This type of plan assumes that the patient is going to pay the doctor when services are rendered.

Then there's the policy that bypasses the patient and sends the check directly to the doctor. For the provider, this is a sort of good news/bad news option. The good news, of course, is that the physician receives direct payment; the bad news is that the doctor is paid in accordance with what the carrier considers *usual and customary* fees, which might not necessarily be what the doctor considers fair compensation.

To make matters more complicated—or more interesting, if you're a glass-half-full instead of half-empty type—various policies limit coverage to various disorders or types of service. Some might not cover maternity services, others might exclude mental disorders, and still others might not allow treatment by chiropractors, optometrists, or dentists.

The Big Three

There are three main types of commercial health insurance plans.

1. *Basic.* These plans pay total costs up to a maximum (usually around $5,000) for all but a few exclusions such as cosmetic surgery and mental disorders. They might or

► I'll Have the Usual

In the cozy world of the coffee shop or diner, "the usual" means what the customer always orders. In the often obtuse world of health insurance, "the usual" is something different. Usual, customary, and reasonable (UCR) refers to a method of regulating health-care costs. Under the UCR method, insurers pay providers as little as they can, or rather, the lesser of these three schedules:

► *Usual fee.* The usual or normal amount doctors charge for a specific service. This figure is determined by insurers who keep annual tabs and then compute an average fee.

► *Customary fee.* This one is determined by insurers based on 90 percent of the fees charged by all doctors in the same specialty in the same geographic region.

► *Reasonable fee.* Here we have the least of: a) the fee the doctor has actually billed, b) the usual fee, c) the customary fee, or d) some other specially justifiable fee.

Another even more complicated method of determining fees is the RBRVS, which, in English, is the Resource-Based Relative Value Scale. Developed by the Harvard School of Public Health, the RBRVS uses all of the following items to come up with a reasonable charge: a) the actual amount of work performed by the doctor; b) the doctor's expenses, excluding malpractice insurance; and c) the cost of malpractice insurance.

Now, just in case you thought that was easy, the RBRVS system multiplies each of these items by an index based on geographic areas and then multiplies the total by a conversion factor decided upon by Congress to account for inflation.

How did Congress get in there? The system was developed at the federal government's behest as a response to Medicare's runaway expenditures.

---

might not have a deductible. Costs can be incurred in the hospital, at the doctor's office, or at home.

2. *Major medical.* These policies are designed for catastrophic situations such as extended hospitalization, which might give you another major medical catastrophe if you saw the bill and didn't have the insurance coverage. They don't pay for minor health problems or office visits, and they almost always feature large deductibles and co-payments.

3. *Comprehensive.* These plans, the combo plate on the commercial carrier's menu, are composites of both basic and major medical coverage.

The Blues

Blue Cross and Blue Shield are the hallmarks of American prepaid health-care coverage. They have been in existence, in one form or another, since the teens of the 20th century. Together, they now provide health insurance coverage to more than one in three Americans, more than 106 million people.

According to the Blue Cross–Blue Shield, the group offers a variety of products including plans for a preferred provider organization (PPO), health maintenance organization (HMO), indemnity (also referred to as point-of-service), flexible spending accounts (FSA), health savings accounts (HSA), and Medicaid. Blue Cross–Blue Shield is the largest single processor of Medicare claims in the United States. Needless to say, every MIB should be very familiar with the BCBSA's role in the health-care system.

stat fact

Since the Affordable Care Act went into effect, the HHS estimates that 5.7 million young adults (aged 19–25) have been able to stay on their parents' health insurance plans until age 26. This is more than double the amount of young folks retaining coverage in previous years.

Blue Cross was originally developed to pay hospitalization costs, while Blue Shield's purpose was to pay for doctors' services. Now, both "brands," as the parent organization likes to call them, have in most states merged into a single entity, the Blue Cross–Blue Shield System.

Blue Cross came along in 1929 when Justin Ford Kimball, an official at Baylor University in Dallas, Texas, ushered in a plan to give schoolteachers 21 days of hospital care for just $6 a year. (The current equivalent would be about $35 a year.)

Other employee groups in Dallas decided the teachers were onto a good thing and jumped on the bandwagon. The idea quickly attracted attention nationwide.

The program snowballed from there, adopting the Blue Cross symbol in 1939, the same year the first modern Blue Shield plan was founded in California. In ten years, the plan grew from 1,300 participants to 3 million. Now, in the second decade of the new millennium, the Blue Cross–Blue Shield System is one of the largest employers in the United States, processes the most hospital and physician contracts, sells insurance to all sectors of the health-care market; and offers 39 plans in all 50 states, the District of Columbia, and Puerto Rico.

Those Dang Deductibles

The *deductible* is the amount the patient must pay before the insurance coverage kicks in. If the policy specifies a $500 deductible, for example, and the patient racks up $600 worth of medical expenses, the carrier will pay toward the last $100, leaving the patient to take care of the balance. If the patient is a basically healthy type and never reaches the $500 mark, the insurance company isn't going to cough up a dime.

Most policies have an *allowable* amount for covered services. This means the insurer pays a portion—usually 70 to 80 percent—of the doctor's fee, and the patient pays the balance, which is called the *co-payment* or *co-insurance*. If the policy above has a $500 deductible and the allowable amount is 80 percent, the insurance carrier will pay $80 of the total $600 bill. (And you thought you were through with word problems!)

In deference to the insured who's having a run of poor health, many policies also include a stop-loss provision, which limits the total co-payments the policy holder must make in a given year. Once the insured has paid $1,000 in co-payments, for example, the

▶ Split Personality

When a patient is covered under two or more health insurance policies, he is said to have dual coverage. This phenomenon is not unusual, especially in today's both-spouses-bringing-home-the-bacon families. Here are some tips on the twin policy front:

▶ *Group plans.* Group health insurance plans usually include a *coordination of benefits* clause. Also known as *nonduplication of benefits*, this provision states that when a patient is covered by more than one group plan, the total benefits paid by all policies are limited to 100 percent of the actual charges.

▶ *Birthday rule.* When a dependent is covered under multiple group plans because both parents have coverage through their employers, the parents' dates of birth are used to determine which coverage is primary, with the older parent's taking first position. Like the old first-aid test question of "Where do you put the tourniquet if the patient has a snake bite on the neck?" you could beg the question of what happens if both parents have the same birth date. You might or might not get an answer.

▶ *Government plans.* If a patient has dual coverage and one of the plans is Medicaid, the government plan is considered supplementary to the private or group plan. Medicare is the major exception here since so many of its insureds also have Medigap coverage. In this case, of course, Medicare is the primary policy. On the other hand, however, for seniors who are still working after age 65 and have both a group and Medicare policy, the group policy counts as the primary.

carrier forgoes any further co-payments and picks up 100 percent of the tab for any and all remaining covered services.

Alphabet Soup

At this point, you might be asking yourself "Just what the heck are HMOs and PPOs?"

HMO stands for *health maintenance organization* and is a sort of privatized version of a national health-care plan. There are various permutations of HMOs, but the gist is that patients pay a monthly fee to belong, much as they would with Blue Cross–Blue Shield. When they need medical care, they present a card like a credit card or library card instead of a claim form. They then see a preassigned physician, called the *primary* physician, within the organization and pay either a nominal fee per visit or no fee at all.

The HMO system insists that the patient see only her primary doctor. She can't choose another doctor within the HMO, and she certainly can't pick one out of the phone book or because Mrs. Hoodle down the street recommended him. HMOs also demand that patients see a specialist only upon the authorization and referral of the primary physician.

The upside of the HMO system is that because the organization is trying to whittle down major medical costs by concurrently whittling away at major medical problems, it will pay for a lot of preventive services (such as well-baby checkups, well-adult physicals, mammograms, and immunizations) that traditional fee-for-service carriers won't cover.

Because of all the taboos, however, HMOs receive a lot of flak from the public, who often feel that their power of choice has been taken away and that the HMO is not providing optimal care. Doctors are not wild about HMOs, either, for the same reasons and for many others, including, of course, money.

Providers who work for HMOs are usually paid on a *capitation* basis. This has nothing to do with decapitating people but stems from the same root word and refers to the practice of counting heads. The HMO decides how many patients the doctor is likely to see in his office in a given month and then pays him for treating that number regardless of how many patients actually cross his threshold.

Regardless, it seems the HMO is here to stay, along with its kissing cousin, the *PPO*, or *preferred provider organization*. This is a group of doctors who cooperate with an insurance plan by accepting fee-for-service payments at less than the usual and customary rate. Unlike most of their HMO brethren, PPO doctors are allowed to see nonplan patients and charge their own fees. PPO patients are granted more autonomy as well and can choose a doctor outside the plan, although they then have to pay a larger chunk of the bill.

High-deductible health plans (HDHPs) feature higher deductibles ($1,000 to $10,000) than traditional insurance plans and are growing in popularity because of their lower premiums. Combining them with a health savings account (HSA) or health reimbursement arrangement (HRA) will help policy holders pay for out-of-pocket medical expenses with pre-tax dollars.

Swimming around in the alphabet soup of *managed care organizations* are a bevy of other crossbreeds. There is the *IPA*, or *independent practice association*; the *EPO*, or *exclusive provider organization*; the *POS*, or *point-of-service plan*; and the *MSO*, otherwise known as the *managed services organization*.

So long as you don't confuse MSO with MSG or IPA with the IRA, you should be able to wade your way through this lot. As with all other insurance plans, the important thing to be aware of is what and how the particular plan pays the physician.

Muddling Through Medicare

Medicare began in 1965 as a star player in President Lyndon B. Johnson's "Great Society," which stemmed from his belief that every American should be able to partake of our nation's wealth. The federal government's gift to older Americans in the form of health insurance, Medicare is available to almost everyone who has reached the grand age of 65. Younger people who suffer from end-stage renal disease (ESRD) and/or have been collecting Social Security disability benefits for more than two years are also eligible.

The Social Security Administration handles Medicare enrollment and premium collection, but the program itself is run by CMS (the agency, not the form). Keep in mind, however, that claims billing is handled by various commercial carriers such as the Blues, called *intermediaries*, and that these carriers vary among states.

Medicare consists of two parts: the "Original Medicare Plan" and the "Medicare Advantage Plan," which are broken into four categories: Parts A, B, C, and D.

1. *Part A.* Provides inpatient hospital services including skilled nursing facilities, hospices, and home health care.
2. *Part B.* Covers doctors' services, outpatient care, and other nonhospitalization services.
3. *Part C.* Private insurance plan that provides both Parts A and B.
4. *Part D.* Reduced-cost prescription plan.

Everyone who has worked, or whose spouse has worked, in Medicare-covered employment or self-employment (basically everybody who had taxes deducted from

▶ Back to HMOs

Most Medicare beneficiaries who belong to HMOs do not bother their little heads with Medicare's deductibles or co-insurance amounts (although they still make co-payments to the HMO), and they still receive all the perks of Medicare coverage. But—and this is a big but—the HMO to which they belong probably has a cost contract with Medicare, which means there are lock-in requirements, which, in turn, means that the Medicare patient is locked into receiving all her care from that particular HMO. Medicare will not pay for any services from any outside source unless it's during an emergency or while the patient is away from the plan's service area.

If the patient belongs to a POS, or point-of-service type of HMO, he probably has enrolled under a *cost plan.* In this case, he is allowed to go to providers outside the managed care plan, and Medicare will pay its share of the bill. In this case, however, the patient is responsible for Medicare's co-insurance and deductibles.

The savvy MIB keeps all these factors in mind when billing for Medicare providers. It's complicated, but it can be fun, too. It's all a game, and the more you know, the more you can win for your doctors, as well as for their patients.

their pay) for at least ten years is entitled to freebie Part A coverage. Those who don't qualify for the freebie. For example, people under age 65 who are disabled but no longer receive disability benefits because of their earnings, can often purchase Part A coverage.

Everyone entitled to Part A is also entitled to Part B—for a price. The monthly premium is usually deducted directly from the insured's monthly Social Security check. There is also a yearly deductible for Part B coverage, after which Medicare pays a percentage of the approved amount for all covered services and the patient pays the remaining percent, or co-insurance.

Part C is called the "Medicare Advantage Plan" and combines Parts A and B. This coverage is provided through private insurance companies that have been approved by Medicare and often has extra benefits. Part D is a premium-based plan that covers medically necessary drugs and is available to anyone enrolled in Parts A, B, or C.

Part B Particulars

The most important thing to remember about Part B coverage is that it covers doctor's bills, no matter where they're incurred—at home, in the doctor's office, in a clinic, or even, presumably, on the golf course. The doctor's fees for services rendered in the hospital or nursing home are also covered here, as opposed to Part A coverage for the charges from the hospital or nursing home itself.

Part B also covers the following:

- ► Outpatient hospital services
- ► X-rays and diagnostic tests
- ► Certain ambulance services
- ► Durable medical equipment used at home, such as wheelchairs and hospital beds
- ► Services of certain nonphysician practitioners
- ► Physical and occupational therapy
- ► Speech/language pathology services
- ► Partial hospitalization for mental health care
- ► Mammograms and Pap smears
- ► Some home health care

For would-be Draculas, Part B covers blood after the patient has met the annual deductible of three pints. It usually doesn't cover outpatient prescription drugs, but it makes an exception for some oral anticancer drugs, certain drugs for hospice patients, and those that are administered as part of the doctor's services. It also covers various drugs given in the first year after transplant surgery, epoetin for home dialysis patients, antigens, and flu, pneumococcal and hepatitis B vaccines.

Accepting Assignment

If all of the above brings back awful memories of your high school algebra book, don't panic. It's a lot to swallow now, but as you flex your MIB wings and use your skills, Medicare's little rules will become second nature.

Feeling better? Good—because now we need to discuss more math, aka "Fun with Accepting Assignment."

The amount Medicare will pay for a covered service is the lesser of two evils, err, the lesser of two prices: Medicare's preapproved amount or the amount charged by the provider. For example, let's say Medicare allows $100 for a simple wart removal. Let's also say Dr. Whosit, who likes to call his own shots, thinks his wart removal services are worth more.

Now, if Dr. Whosit accepts assignment from Medicare—meaning he will accept Medicare's approved wart fee as his full payment—he bills Medicare for $100. Medicare sends a check for $80 (80 percent of $100) directly to him, and he bills the patient for the remaining $20, which is the other 20 percent, or co-insurance amount. End of story.

If, on the other hand, Dr. Whosit does not accept assignment, he bills the patient $115. Why this amount? Because doctors who do not accept assignment are allowed to charge up to 15 percent more than the Medicare-approved amount and no more. This is referred to as the *limiting charge*.

By law, Dr. Whosit must also send a bill to Medicare on the patient's behalf, but Medicare will send the payment—which is still only $80 (Medicare's 80 percent of the approved $100 amount)—to the patient. The patient will then remember that he owes this $80, plus the remaining $35, to Dr. Whosit and fire off a check.

Now, let's say Dr. Whosit's brother, Dr. Whatsit, does his wart removals for only $80 a pop. Medicare will

 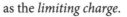

▶ Benefit Basics

An EOB is an *explanation of benefits* and is the insurance carrier's method of summarizing the details of the claim submitted and explaining the particulars of reimbursement. Although each payer can define benefits in its own endearingly idiosyncratic way, you can expect to find essentially the same information on any EOB:

- ▶ Patient's name and relationship to insured

- ▶ Services rendered, dates of service, and total charges

- ▶ Exclusions and special (not sarcastic, although it may seem that way) remarks about the reason for denial, suspended claims, or additional information needed

- ▶ Amount of total charges covered

- ▶ Deductible amounts due for each service

- ▶ Percentage of allowed balance paid

- ▶ Required provider adjustments or other deductions

pay $64, which is 80 percent of $80, and Dr. Whatsit can bill his patient $16, which is the remaining 20 percent. Got it? Good.

Now, one more interesting twist. Let's say Dr. Whosit has a colleague, Dr. Frankenstein. And let's say Dr. Frank is running a laboratory (as in diagnostic lab testing). Medicare will require Dr. Frank to accept assignment—he has no choice in the matter.

As a last aside, you should know that doctors decide each year whether or not to take the plunge and accept assignment. If they do, they become a *PAR* or *participating physician* (guess Medicare decided the acronym PP wouldn't be too appealing). If they decline, they become a *non-PAR*.

Oh, That Medigap!

Many people purchase supplemental health-care insurance to cover co-insurance fees. This supplemental coverage is referred to as *Medigap* because it fills in the gaps between what Medicare pays and what it doesn't.

Medigap insurance is sold and administered by private carriers, but it is regulated by both state and federal laws. There are ten standard plans, lettered A through N (Note: E, H, I, and J are no longer available to new subscribers). Plan A is the basic package and must be offered, although purchasers can upgrade to a different plan, with Plans C and F being the most popular.

Medigap policies cover all, or nearly all, co-insurance amounts. Some cover deductibles. Others pay doctor charges that exceed the approved amount, and still others take care of otherwise noncovered services such as prescription drugs and preventive screenings (the health-care kind, not the Hollywood movie kind).

Let's go back to Dr. Whosit and let's say he's accepting Medicare assignment. Let's say that you, his ace medical biller, put the patient's Medigap policy number on the Medicare claim and send it in. Medicare will process the claim and then automatically forward it to the Medigap carrier, which will process the claim and send a check directly to Dr. Whosit.

Even keener, some Medigap insurers have *cross-over contracts* with Medicare. In these cases, Medicare will automatically forward claims even if the doctor does not accept assignment.

Medicaid

The Medicaid program is designed to provide health-care coverage for people residing at or near the poverty level—people who could not otherwise afford any health care at all. The Patient Protection and Affordable Care Act has since revised and expanded the eligibility and enrollment requirements for Medicaid recipients. This includes extending funding for the Children's Health Insurance Program (CHIP).

> **tip**
>
> *The Medicare Guide* (available from CMS at 800-633-4227 or www. medicare.gov) contains a dandy chart detailing the benefits of each Medigap plan.

Administered jointly by CMS and each state's government, the program has one major flaw—its allowable charges are pitifully low in some states. Many doctors don't accept Medicaid because the cost of doing the paperwork, not to mention the costs of providing the service, exceed the amount they'll be paid.

Some patients have Medicare as their primary coverage and Medicaid as supplemental health-care coverage. These people are called *crossover patients*. Like Medicare, Medicaid claims are processed by private carriers, and these carriers vary among states.

Why You Should Care About Obamacare

The Affordable Care Act (aka Obamacare) is a federal law enacted in 2010 that is intended to provide access to health insurance to individuals, families, and small businesses; to reduce health-care costs; and limit insurance companies' ability to deny, rescind, or restrict coverage. It has also created a lot more jobs in medical billing claims industry.

With an increased number of insured people, and companies required to cover those with pre-existing conditions and those older in age, there has been a boom in enrollment. This has raised the number of people seeing a doctor, and in turn has increased the medical billing services needed. Before ACA, four in ten adults claimed they did not go to the doctor when they knew they needed it because they lacked insurance. Now, those four in ten can go whenever they need.

stat fact

Another impact of ACA is the growth in medical billing professionals. In 2015, the Bureau of Labor Statistics projected that the industry would grow by 22 percent between now and 2022.

Of course, not all is golden. The Affordable Care Act (or ACA) has raised questions about the impact on various levels of the population, including the medical claims billing industry. At its legislative introduction, the ACA increased the number of people who had access to medical care, which in turn increased the amount of medical claims billing required. This was aggravated by the fact that ACA required health-care professionals to restructure how they handled medical billing components in the form of the ICD-10 medical billing codes. This process has not been fun.

Reimbursement rates and allowances for patients have also been changed. Now, almost all insurance plans have changed coverage. These changes have been taxing on medical claims billing professionals because they are the ones who communicate with insurance companies and patients to ensure proper coverage. The Minnesota MIB says that some insurance companies are still having trouble getting their computer systems to pay correctly, and this is resulting in more and more claims not being paid or denied incorrectly, which results in more work for the biller. "The ACA has been an issue for all medical providers to billers/coders and anyone else involved in medical billing," says Sandra S.

In any event, with the influx of new patients, this means that more skilled coding and billing experts are needed to help communicate with insurers and process medical claims for medical providers around the country.

Overall, the Affordable Care Act has changed the professional landscape for the medical industry as much as it has changed the health-care access for citizens. Nowhere is this more apparent among the health-care professions than with medical coders and billers.

TRICARE

Moving right along the government insurance hit parade, we arrive at TRICARE (formerly known as Civilian Health and Medical Program of the Uniformed Services, or CHAMPUS).

► Associating with the Medical Billing Industry

Liz Jones, academic director for the Medical Association of Billers, has some advice for anyone hoping to get involved in the medical billing business—don't quit your day job . . . yet. "To me, you really have to know the different types of insurance," Jones says. "I suggest people work six months to a year in a doctor's office before they start a business." That way, she says, you work and earn money while enjoying a ramp-up period.

Jones knows her stuff, so it's wise to trust her advice. As academic director for the MAB, she helps create programming and learning opportunities for around 1,500 members worldwide. The MAB was founded in 1995 in Las Vegas, and the association website launched in 1997. It was one of the first groups to offer online classes, which they still do, along with facetime learning opportunities. The group's Power Weekends provide medical billers with a two-day refresher course on coding and billing. The MAB also offers on-site training at your place of business, certification training, proctor sites, and a national conference for billing professionals.

"This is a good business, but you have to pay your dues," Jones says. As such, she does not necessarily recommend the "turnkey" approach to starting your own billing service. The software required, she says, is often too complicated for an inexperienced novice to get used to immediately. "It's not as easy as sitting down at the computer and plugging in numbers," she says. There are nuances of each insurance company and each medical office that one must master in order to bill the most money for her clients. So, do your homework first and participate in as many professional activities as you can prior to hanging out your shingle, from working in a medical office to taking a certification class.

Challenges are many for the first-time MIB, the biggest of which is getting that first client. If working full time in a medical office isn't a possibility for you, Jones says to volunteer for a physician's office to see if you enjoy the environment and pace of work. "Most people will spend money [on software] before they get a client. It's a shame to invest that kind of money when you don't even know if you like doing it." Once you do get that first client, focus plenty of energy on recruiting new clients. Jones recommends starting with people you know. One client has a lot of marketing power if he tells his colleagues about his good experience with you, so don't be afraid to ask for referrals. Jones predicts that you will need at least three or four clients to really start bringing in some solid funds. "If you just have one small contractor," she says, "I wouldn't quit your day job."

To find out more about the Medical Association of Billers, visit their website at www. physicianswebsites.com. There, you'll find tons of resources from forms and sample documents to HIPAA information and member forums.

TRICARE provides civilian health-care coverage to active and retired military personnel and their dependents so they can be treated by George Clooney instead of Captain Newman, M.D.

Workers' Compensation

This used to be called work*men's* compensation insurance until gender equality struck. *Workers'* compensation provides private insurance coverage for both males and females who become injured or ill while on the job and can encompass everything from a knock on the noggin with a steel beam to stress-related mental illness.

Every employer with more than a specific number of employees is required by law to carry workers' compensation insurance, which is provided—at a staggering price—by various private carriers.

Workers' comp cases are handled differently from most other insurance claims. Sometimes it's unclear if the case even is a workers' comp matter. For example, an employee involved in an auto accident may have been tootling around in the company car on her off time, or a stress-related problem may stem from a tyrannical spouse instead of the boss from hell. In such an instance, second-opinion reviews may be required. This can also occur in cases involving a dispute about the level of disability.

Treatment must be preauthorized (the insurance carrier must be called while the patient bleeds onto the emergency room floor, unless, of course, it's after hours for the insurer, in which case a call is put in as soon after treatment as possible). After treatment, the provider must fill out lots of other fun forms, such as the Initial Medical Report and the First Report of Injury. These reports must include the case number and the adjuster's name.

Fee allowances are set by the state and paid directly to the doctor by the insurance carrier.

The End, Finito

There are so many rules, regulations, permutations, and ins and outs in insurance coverage that this chapter could easily stretch on forever.

What we have provided should give you a good basic grounding in Insurance 101. The rest you can learn in several ways:

▶ *Immerse yourself.* There is no better way to learn than by throwing yourself into the deep end.

▶ *Send away for stuff.* Remember when you were a kid and you sent away for free stuff out of magazines, just to get something in the mail? Well, you can still do it. Only now you can send away for stuff that you really need, such as the *Medicare Guide*. We have provided a list of helpful goodies you can use in the Appendix.

▶ *Ask for help.* Answers are out there for the asking. Develop a network of MIB buddies. Get on the internet with everybody from fellow billers to the Blues. Go to your business opportunity or software vendor.

▶ *Demand answers.* There's no better source for answers than the problem itself. You can always call Medicare or Blue Cross or the TRICARE carrier and tell them what you need to know. Ask nicely—but firmly.

Day-to-Day Operations

N ow that you are versed in the ins and outs and whys and wherefores of health insurance, let's take a look at operations. In this chapter, we explore what an MIB's work life is really like, what sorts of tasks you can expect to perform on a daily basis, and how they are completed. If Chapter 1 was akin to investigative reports, then Chapter 3 is a text-only version of all those big coffee-table books called *A Day in the Life of Spam or Delaware: An Intimate Portrait*. You know, the ones that show every facet of the subject's life from rising at dawn to feed the chickens to midnight fireworks over the Capitol.

As a rule, MIBs don't actually dabble in animal husbandry, but since many are stay-at-home moms as well as business owners, they do often rise at dawn's early light to do a little work before feeding their hungry chicks. Our version of *A Day in the Life* won't feature midnight "fireworks"—but we will peer into nightly routines and rituals.

Good Morning, Medical Biller!

One of the great joys of running a medical billing service is that you can arrange your workload around any schedule you choose. Some MIBs are early birds, catching those worms; others find they get more accomplished in the afternoon or at night. The hours they spend and the time frames within which they structure those hours are as individual as each entrepreneur.

"The funniest thing," says an MIB in New Jersey, and the mother of two, "is that most people who are trying to get in the business and have talked to me, really want me to answer the question as to how many hours a day I work. I just can never answer that because I don't know."

She may have 20 minutes to sit down, undisturbed, she explains, before she may be called upon to get up, fix lunch, and get the kids off to school. Then she can come back and work for an hour, but something always comes up. "It's never-ending," she says.

"Of course, [my daily schedule is] always changing," says the former nurse/MIB in San Diego who's also a mother of two. "I tend to get up early in the morning because that is my peace-and-quiet time. So I'm usually up by 5:30 in the morning, in my office by 6:00."

If your eyes roll back in your head at the idea of rising before *Good Morning America* appears on the tube, don't panic. This is not an industry must. "My mornings are pretty much my most hectic time," the New Jersey MIB explains. She does the mommy stuff in between taking client calls and fielding problems. "Most of my clients pretty much know my schedule, and they know that the mornings are for troubleshooting."

She breaks near noon for lunch, bundles the kids off to kindergarten and day care, then, she says, "I pretty much have from 12:30 P.M. to 4:00 P.M. where I can really sit and work."

warning

When you work at home, friends and family can monopolize your time, dropping in for a cup of coffee and a chat because "you're home anyway." Be polite but firm. Let them know you're at the office and need to buckle down to business.

Practice Particulars

What, specifically, you will be doing during your peak hours and beyond will depend on how you've structured your services. Some MIBs perform *full practice management* for their clients—they handle all aspects of the doctor's accounting from submitting electronic claims to billing patients to tracking accounts payable and receivable. Other medical billers prefer to deal only with insurance claims submissions. Most MIBs, being savvy businesspeople, take on whatever is required to land the client and therefore find themselves working in different ranges of practice management for different clients.

► The How-To Revue

Here's the Radio City Rockettes' chorus line of chores, a sort of rapid-fire revue of an MIB's daily bump and grind:

1. Enter your patient information, adding new insurance carriers to your database as you go along. Be sure you enter the referral source or referring physician as well as any other information you've agreed to track for your clients.

2. Enter CPT and ICD-10 codes from the superbills and day sheets. Your software will automatically fill in the amounts charged for each procedure. Enter each charge on a separate line.

3. Transmit electronic claims directly to insurance carriers or to the clearinghouse.

4. Receive audit report, review, and correct errors on audit report, forward clean claims, and resubmit rejected claims.

5. Print any paper claims. Separate claims into your copy and the insurer's, fold, and insert in envelopes. Weigh any envelopes containing more than five claims to make sure you have sufficient postage.

6. Post payments to each patient's account. Most software programs include features that show which charges have been paid, how much is left on each charge, and which charges are still unpaid.

7. Print aging reports so you can review each patient's account to determine which ones haven't been paid in a timely manner. Most software packages will do this for you, too.

8. Call insurance carriers to check on the status of delinquent claims. Most of your follow-up calls will be for paper claims.

9. Put your feet up and relax. You've earned a breather.

"I'm kind of an à la carte," the Denver MIB says of the services she offers. "[The doctors] just tell me what kind of services they need. That's what I try to provide, and then I charge them accordingly."

Mary V. discovered that smaller practices, those with one or two doctors at the helm, have no business background and desperately need assistance. "I don't like to say full-practice management," Mary says of the accounting services she offers these small practices, "because we're not in that office. We call it accounts receivable management."

In western Virginia, Kim H. prefers to stick to claims billing, but she also does patient billing for two of her four providers simply because they requested the service. Her reasoning? "I didn't want to turn them down."

The Nitty-Gritty

Most software packages are equipped to handle as many billing tasks as you care to take on. In addition to claims billing and patient accounting, many allow you to spew out a dazzling variety of reports and graphs. You can chart each provider's income by type of insurance carrier or by how much income she's derived from each referring physician. You can also punch out all the normal sorts of accounting reports.

The Denver MIB provides each of her doctors with a monthly report, which she breaks down between office and hospital production or between inpatient and outpatient services. The report details all the doctor's procedures and how many times those procedures were performed, then goes on to chart collections, which she breaks down into special categories such as medical records copying, legal arbitrations, and depositions.

No matter how esoteric you want to get, your most basic task will be generating and transmitting insurance claims. Software makes this part a snap. Although each program has its own variations, the basic setup is the same, featuring a screen or screens where you enter the patient's particulars, including name, phone, address, policy number, date of injury or illness, the diagnosis and procedure codes, and the doctor's charges.

When you first take on a practice, you'll spend a fair number of hours entering all the doctor's patients into your program. Although this is a time-consuming kickoff, it's well worth the effort—afterward you'll always have most of the information you'll need on file. Unless established patients move or change employers or insurance companies, all you'll need to fill in are the details of the illness or injury, the diagnosis and procedure codes, and the charges. The basics—name, address, phone, employer, policy number(s), insured family member's name and relationship, your own file or ID number for the patient—are already entered.

Sometimes the diagnosis portion is pretty simple, too. Chiropractors, for example, tend to treat the same problem for an extended period, so once you have Patient Peterson down for a wrenched back diagnosis, that code will remain the same until the patient finishes his course of treatment.

► Insurer, May I?

Insurance carriers often require providers to obtain precertification before they'll agree to pay for certain hospital admissions, inpatient or outpatient surgeries, and elective procedures (ones not requiring immediate action). Precertification was designed to reduce health-care costs by reducing or eliminating unnecessary services; therefore, the doctor must inform the carrier of the medical service planned and receive permission before forging ahead.

Most Medicaid programs have rigid precertification requirements for all nonemergency hospitalizations and surgeries. Most commercial plans now follow suit, insisting on pre-certification for nonemergency hospitalizations and for specific surgical procedures such as tonsillectomies.

As an added bonus, many carriers require the doctor to produce a second opinion before they'll approve the procedure or course of treatment. Some offer employers reduced premiums in return for revised plans that include some precertification clauses.

With more than 1,000 commercial and government carriers out there, you can't know every stipulation for every carrier. You'll learn by trial and error and from others' experiences.

Offer your doctors a "Precertification Form" to use in their practices. This is a great marketing technique, as well as smart business sense. It shows your clients your knowledge and efficiency while it streamlines operations.

You can copy the form in Figure 3–1, page 46 or modify it to meet your clients' specific needs. Why not customize it with your business name or your doctors'?

When precertification is necessary, be sure the doctor's office fills out a copy of the form and has it available when calling the carrier. If the carrier won't precertify a procedure over the phone, your client can fax or mail it with a cover letter. Or you can add this to the list of services you provide.

You'll want to be sure to get a copy of the completed precertification form with the preauthorization number filled in so that you can enter that number on the patient's claim form.

Precertification Form

Preauthorization number: _____

Insurance carrier: _____

Certification for admission: _____ Procedure: _____

Patient's name: _____

Date of birth: _____ Phone no.: _____

Street address: _____

City/state/zip: _____

Subscriber's name: _____

Address if different from patient's: _____

_____

Member no.: _____ Group no.: _____

Provider name: _____ Provider ID no.: _____

Provider address: _____

Provider phone: _____ Contact name: _____

Hospital or facility: _____

Planned admission/procedure date: _____

Estimated length of stay: _____

Diagnosis/symptoms: _____

Treatment/procedure: _____

Complicating factors: _____

Second opinion required?: _____ If yes, obtained?: _____

Corroborating physician: _____

Insurance carrier rep.: _____

Approval?: _____

If no, reason for denial: _____

FIGURE 3–1: **Precertification Form**

Secret Decoder Ring

At this point you might be thinking "Gee, swell! Except where in the heck do I get the codes?"

Not to worry. You'll find the procedure and diagnosis codes, otherwise known as the *CPT* (for *Current Procedural Terminology*) and *ICD-10* (for *International Classification of Diseases, 10th revision* and most properly called *ICD-10-CM*, for *Clinical Modification*)

▶ Fun with CPT Codes

CPT codes are divided into three categories, with Category I being the most widely used in the medical industry. This category incorporates most of the procedures performed by health-care providers for inpatient and outpatient care. Category II codes are supplemental tracking codes used to report performance and quality measures. Category III codes are temporary codes used for defining experimental and emerging technology, services, and procedures.

Since Category I is the group you will be playing in the most often, we will identify the six sections specifying a different branch of medicine, each containing hundreds of different procedures.

Anesthesia:	00100–01999; 99100–99140
Surgery:	10021–69990
Radiology:	70010–79999
Pathology and Laboratory:	80047–89398
Medicine:	90281–99199; 99500–99607
Evaluation and Management:	99201–99499

The Evaluation and Management, or E&M, section is used to categorize types of visits by setting: office, hospital, home, clinic, nursing home, golf course, etc. These visits are further categorized by type of patient—new (one never before seen or one not seen in at least three years) or established—length of visit; complexity of visit; type of decision making involved in the visit; and the list goes on.

We won't run down every permutation here, but you should glance over these codes to get an idea of what exactly is involved so that when you see them on the superbill, you'll know what you're looking at. Take note, however, that all codes are subject to revisions. The only way to know exactly what is what is to make sure your coding books and software are up to date and to keep abreast of Medicare bulletins.

codes, on the superbill. Some MIBs prefer to set their doctors up with day sheets, a sort of running superbill list of each patient the doctor sees on a particular day (see Figure 3–2, page 49 for a sample day sheet).

Proper procedure codes are one of the most important parts of any insurance claim—they tell the carrier exactly what services or procedures were performed and/or what supplies were provided. Procedure coding can be extremely complex and in some cases has been elevated to the level of detailed craftsmanship. Hospitals and some large practices with in-house billers have employees who do nothing but coding. Coding requires a considerable knowledge of medical terminology, operative procedures, and other aspects of clinical medicine.

There are, for example, more than ten different codes to describe an office visit. Which code is used depends on whether the patient is new to the practice and also on the level of service provided. Think of it this way: A new patient requires more time than the old pal of the practice who's been seen twice a month for the past two years for the same medical problem. Dr. Whynot will want to spend time with New Patient Pamela, establishing a relationship, determining exactly what Pam's problem is, and working out a course of treatment. When Old Pal Peterson arrives in the office, however, Dr. Whynot can stick her head in, briefly inquire about any developments, and then leave the patient in the capable hands of her assistant for the routine treatment.

Think, too, of the differences between two types of emergency visits. There's every mother's nightmare, the head-wound-gushing-blood-that-needs-stitches, and then we have the handyman special, stepped-on-a-nail-in-the-garage-and-needs-a-tetanus-shot. In the first instance, Dr. Whynot needs to spend quite a bit of time with the patient, making sure there's no concussion involved and reviving fainting parents, in addition to suturing the wound. In the second instance, Handy Dan pops in, Dr. Whynot glances at his heel, determines that it's not infected, and bustles on to her next patient while her nurse stabs Dan with the tetanus needle.

You can see the time difference in these two types of visits. You can also see the difference in billable procedures. The first will involve a charge for an extended office visit, a charge for suturing the wound, and possibly another charge for a tetanus injection. There might also be a charge for tranquilizers for Mum. Handy Dan, on the other hand, will be charged for a brief office visit (or maybe none at all) and the injection.

The fees charged for the various office visits can be anywhere from $25 to $250, and insurance carriers—no dummies—are not going to pay $250 for the Handy Dan version. You can see why some MIBs feel so strongly that you should have a medical background before embarking on your business.

Day Sheet

Day Sheet Page _____ of _____ Date _____ Day _____

File #	Patient	Services	DX A/C	Charges	Payments	Balance Forward
1						
2						
3						
4						
5						
6						
7						
8						
9						
10						
11						
12						
13						
14						
15						
16						
17						
18						
19						
20						
21						
22						
23						
24						
25						
26						
27						
28						
29						
30						

FIGURE 3–2: **Day Sheet**

The column marked "DX A/C" can be translated as "diagnosis add or change" and is filled in when the patient is new to the practice or when his diagnosis changes. When a patient is first seen for a back strain, for example, the office staff fills in the correct ICD-10 code. On all successive visits for the same injury, the column is left blank. If the patient is subsequently treated for a new problem, the new code is filled in.

But again, don't panic. As a billing service, you are neither required—nor allowed—to provide or change a code for a medical procedure or office visit. That's the provider's job.

Most doctors specialize. Even good ol' GPs (general practitioners) specialize in basic illnesses—colds, the flu, conjunctivitis (pinkeye to you), simple lacerations, and sprained ankles. Anything out of their realm they send on to someone else. Other doctors do the same: Urologists refer to neurologists, cardiologists to oncologists. The point here is that each provider's superbill will consist of one page of procedures and diagnoses, each of which he's familiar with. As you work with his superbills, you'll become familiar with them as well.

tip

Tipping off your doctors to new coding techniques is a darn good marketing technique. It shows them that you are actively increasing their revenues in ways they might not have discovered for themselves. Remember, you have the secret decoder ring!

Incidentally, you might find it interesting—and sobering—to know that the National Center for Health Statistics approved 15 new codes to classify a death or an injury as terrorist-related following the events of September 11, 2001.

Verify and Clarify

The more you know about coding, the more help you can be to your doctors—and to yourself. It goes without saying that the more money you make for the doctor, the more you make for yourself.

You can't legally take your trusty red pen, cross out the doctor's codes, and substitute those you think are more interesting. You can, however, guide your providers toward in-the-know billing techniques.

The San Diego MIB says that when she finds incorrect codes on her clients' day sheets, she shoots them off a quick email clarifying what the code should actually read. "I'm assisting with the coding, but I'm technically not the coder. But I know what the basics are and what should be there and what shouldn't be there, so what I do is just verify and clarify with the office."

"It's not a matter of just entering the numbers that are on the sheet," the Denver MIB explains. "What I find with my physicians is that they know what they've done—they just don't know how to express it on a superbill. Because I can say to my doctor, 'OK, you did this procedure. Did you do a follow-up telephone call on it? Did you know you can combine that with your next visit and you can get paid for that?' And the doctors [respond], 'I can?'

"Actually, when I get a new doctor I do a superbill evaluation for them so that I can see what kind of codes they're using and which codes are no longer in use. Then I just give them tidbits now and then from seminars that I attend, let them know that 'Gee, I learned you can do this,' or 'I learned something about this procedure code.'"

She tries to do some revamping of the superbills each provider has been using. Most have reprinted their superbills based on what they've learned from her. But her doctor training doesn't stop there.

"Make sure that you are really specific about this code for me," she says in illustration of how she instructs her doctors. "I just pass on different things to them, such as modifiers and when they can use them and when to let me know that they've done something that I can tack a modifier on and get them more money—or get them paid in the first place."

> **warning** ⚠
>
> Be certain that what you're doing is updating your doctors to the latest techniques, not telling them how to code. This is their territory and their responsibility. Make sure you keep all superbills, day sheets, or other materials to back up that what you've entered on a claim came from the provider's hand.

▶ Don't Fool with Fraud

The National Health Care Anti-Fraud Association (NHCAA) reports a loss of 3 to 10 percent of total health-care costs to fraud, which amounts to about $100 billion dollars per year. Some groups even estimate the cost to be higher at around 10 percent, or $170 billion. To counteract this staggering sum, CMS teamed up with the FBI and other investigative agencies to seek out and destroy fraudulent providers. According to a report from HGS Administrators, a Medicare carrier with facilities in Delaware, New Jersey, Pennsylvania, and Virginia, fraudulent acts include these types of creative exercises:

> ▶ Billing for services or supplies that were not performed, provided, or requested

> ▶ Billing for noncovered services as if they were covered

> ▶ Misrepresenting diagnoses

> ▶ Sending in false claims

> ▶ Paying fees for patient referrals

> ▶ Altering claim forms and records

In the Groove

The CPT codes are revised every year, which means you need to stay up-to-date. When you take on a new client, you should—like the Denver MIB—grade his or her current superbill. Does it contain the latest ICD-10 codes specific to that practice? If not, recommend changes. You're asking for trouble if you use outdated codes. The chances are great that the carrier won't pay the same on an old code; in fact, it may refuse to recognize it. Either way, reimbursement won't be swift, and you won't look good.

But let's not look on the grim side. Let's say you review your new client's codes and suggest changes. Right away, you've presented yourself as someone knowledgeable in her field. You send in claims

warning

Remember that CPT codes are revised annually. Don't skip a year. If you do, you could provide yourself with hours of awful torture trying to determine which changes made during the previous year apply to your clients' superbills.

▶ Leveling the CPT Codes

Unraveling the mysteries of procedure codes can seem as daunting as trying to decode a World War I secret spy message. But if you think they're baffling now, be glad you weren't starting out any time before 1983, when Medicare and HCFA developed the current system. During those Dark Ages of medical coding, there were more than 120 different coding systems floating around the United States.

The current system is the brainchild of the American Medical Association, which updates it each year, and is divided into three levels, sort of like the consecutively deeper levels of a top-secret underground military installation. The entire package is called the *Health Care Common Procedure Coding System*, or *HCPCS*, which those in the know pronounce as "Hick-Pix."

The top level—the one used most often—is called the *CPT-4* (for *Current Procedural Terminology*) and contains more than 7,000 codes that are updated yearly. These are the codes that describe the doctor's services, procedures, and visits.

Level II comes next. Level II codes are concerned with durable medical equipment, medical supplies such as gauze and syringes, chemotherapy, and a host of miscellaneous services.

The bottom level and—to follow our secret underground facility analogy—therefore the most obscure, is *HCPCS Local Level III*. These codes are used on a local level by Medicare offices in different states to describe new procedures that only they might recognize.

with up-to-date codes. The doctor—who obviously didn't even realize he was working with outmoded material—is reimbursed in record time. You're a savior!

This might be another point where you've gotten up to refill your coffee mug, come back and muttered, "Did I miss something while I was interfacing with Mr. Coffee? Just how do I get in the groove on all this up-to-date CPT stuff?"

Well, you haven't missed a beat. There are many ways to scope out coding scoops. One way, as the Denver MIB suggests, is to attend coding seminars. Another is to take training provided by reputable medical billing business opportunity vendors. Yet another is to subscribe to—and read—newsletters and bulletins.

Most Medicare and Medicaid carriers provide free seminars explaining how their programs work and supplying valuable billing information. This is an excellent way to increase your knowledge and keep up with the ever-changing requirements. Some organizations will put you on their mailing lists and notify you of classes. Others place only doctors' offices on their lists. In this case, you should try to cultivate a friendship with an office manager and see if you can coast in as a member of her staff. There's no cost, and it's well worth the effort.

Other coding resources are available by surfing the internet. Yahoo Groups has MIB forums where you can either "lurk," reading other people's questions and answers without participating (recommended for the strong, silent—or shy—type), or participate actively, tossing out coding questions to your fellow billers. You'll be amazed at what you can learn in these places. You can subscribe to listservs (online groups) for chiropractors, for example. You can surf government, lobbyist, and corporate-type websites—HCFA, the AMA, Blue Cross-Blue Shield—and pick up information.

Not nearly as exhilarating, but a lot more time-efficient, is yet another source: medical coding books. Optum360, a mail-order house specializing in medical coding books, will happily send you books, spiral binders, software, and even cheat sheets on everything you could ever want to know about coding. (Their mailing address, phone number, and website address, as well as those of other excellent medical text houses, are listed in the Appendix.)

OK, that about wraps it up for CPT codes. But there's more on the secret decoder front. We still have to discuss diagnoses. After all, what's the point in having a procedure code if you don't have a diagnosis to be treated?

The Diagnosis Code Dirt

Diagnosis or ICD-10 codes are developed by the WHO (the World Health Organization, not the rock group). These codes are used internationally to describe accidents, illnesses, and injuries for the purposes of medical research and reporting. This, of course, includes reporting diagnoses to insurance carriers to support the procedure code charge.

The ICD-10 is a modified international standard for diagnosis classifications. The design is intended to improve communication across clinics by capturing data better for risk factors, signs, and symptoms. This is especially important when a patient has two or more illnesses or conditions at the same time (aka "comorbidity"). It also makes it easier for U.S.-based medical clinics to exchange information internationally.

The new codes replaced the old codes effective October 1, 2015, and they are way different from the ICD-9 codes. This new code set is more descriptive and contains up to seven alpha and numeric characters rather than the previously allotted five. In addition, the diagnosis codes for ICD-9 made up roughly 14,000 unique diagnosis codes and 4,000 procedure codes, while the ICD-10 allows for over 69,000 diagnosis codes and 72,000 procedure codes.

In order to be compliant by the deadline, medical facilities and providers scrambled to prepare for the transition by familiarizing themselves with the new codes, preparing their current medical billing with the appropriate ICD-10 codes, and ensuring that any medical

▶ When to Use ICD-9 Codes

Understanding when medical claims billers/coders need to use the ICD-9 codes can be a little tricky. The most important thing to understand is that ICD-9-CM codes are no longer accepted on paper or electronic claims after October 1, 2015. Claims that contain the ICD-9 codes on or after this date are returned to the provider. Do not pass "Go," do not get paid. Billers whose claims are rejected or returned because of an invalid code can correct the issue and resubmit the claims. When this happens a letter of explanation or a Remittance Advice letter will be received, which offers information about the error in question. Once the claim has been fixed, a new claim can be resubmitted within the filing period.

A claim cannot contain codes from ICD-10 and ICD-9. Any claims with both codes will be returned as "unprocessable." Sadly, unprocessable claims cannot be appealed. However, a "reopening" can be requested, which is a separate process from an appeal. Then, once the claim has been corrected it can be resubmitted in timely fashion.

If claims are split for patients whose procedures or services spanned the October 1, 2015, implementation deadline, separate claims will have to be filed for the services provided before the implementation date and after.

billers they hired were qualified to work with the new codes. Needless to say, medical billers and coders had to familiarize themselves quickly with a significantly larger number of codes and more convoluted change processes. There is now greater specificity among coding. All entities which are covered by HIPAA have had to make this transition.

The Denied ICD-10 Code

If a claim is denied because of the diagnosis code, it's usually for one of the following reasons:

- ▶ No diagnosis is provided.
- ▶ The diagnosis given is inconsistent with the service or procedure provided.
- ▶ The diagnosis doesn't substantiate the need or level of service provided.
- ▶ Multiple diagnoses are given, which confuses the claims examiner.

OK! The first two problems are easy to solve. Make sure you have at least one diagnosis for each procedure or group of related procedures, and be sure the diagnosis is consistent with the procedure listed. The insurance company isn't going to pay for a Pap smear when the diagnosis is male pattern baldness.

Moving on to Problem Number 3: If the diagnosis doesn't validate the level of service, then the doctor has probably failed to code for extenuating circumstances. Let's say, for example, that Dr. Whosit billed a two-hour procedure at a three-hour rate. Insurance carriers love to deny claims, and this gives them the perfect opportunity. To get Dr. Whosit paid, you'll need to send an explanation with the charge, making it clear that the procedure took extra time because the patient's diabetes complicated the surgery, or because the patient had an alien like Sigourney Weaver's wedged in his intestines.

Problem Number 4 can also be solved with some vigilance on your part. Many doctors have a tendency to overdiagnose for the purposes of insurance billing, using two, three, or even four different ICD-10 codes to justify a single procedure. In this case, more is not better. All this does is create confusion in the mind of the claims examiner, who will then try to decide which, if any, of the multiple codes submitted justify the procedure—and its payment. Often such claims are either sent back to the doctor for additional information or forwarded to a nurse or physician reviewer.

The rule here is the same one that applies to Army details or IRS audits: Don't volunteer. Don't give them any more to think about than is necessary.

New ICD-10 Codes and Paper Superbills

You may be wondering how the new ICD-10 codes affect paper superbills, whether these superbills are now obsolete, and what is typically used or given to the biller. Although many practices are now entering their services electronically, a large number of medical practices still rely on paper superbills to capture their charge data. Because these are usually small practices with specialties such as dermatology or psychiatry, this method remains fast and efficient.

With the new transition, practitioners who use the paper superbill must use the ICD-10 codes defined for their particular practice, so the superbill can be used for charge capture. Keep in mind that while the number of codes has significantly increased, the patient population for a particular practice probably has not. Physicians today are still treating the same patients they did yesterday, as well as before the October, 1, 2015, deadline. So the superbill needs to only have codes applicable to that practice.

> **tip**
>
> If you need some "face time" with a client without doing so in person, use one of the popular video conferencing applications such as Skype, Google Hangouts, or FaceTime. These free apps can be easily accessed through your laptop, tablet, or smartphone.

The transition to the ICD-10 can be done by finding the ICD-9 code listed on old superbills and converting it to the modified ICD-10 version. In some cases, there is a one-to-one match, and in others there might be a handful of ICD-10 codes that map back to the single ICD-9 code used previously. But with the same patient load and same diagnoses, this is not an overwhelming task. There are GEMs, or General Equivalence Mappings, provided online that give a list of mappings from ICD-9 to ICD-10. These tools make it easy to find the right codes for the new ICD-10 superbills.

Just the Fax, Ma'am

Now that you know all about coding, let's backtrack a bit. How are you going to get the superbills or day sheets to take your CPT and ICD-10 codes from?

Most MIBs rely on one or a combination of four methods: the fax machine, email, personal pickup and delivery, and the USPS. When you make your decision, keep in mind that you'll be dealing with more than just superbills—you'll also have patient information sheets, explanation of benefits (EOBs) from insurance carriers, and correspondence from patients and insurers.

The New Jersey MIB receives her material via fax. "Every once in a while, I'll make a pickup if I'm in the area or if they have an overflow," she says. She cut down on the amount of paper coming through her machine by redesigning her clients' superbills (which, she confesses, "I despise") into day sheets. "If you have 20 patients that day, instead of 20 superbills, I've got one day sheet with all 20 patients and all the information on it."

She compiles each day's faxes and then sorts them into baskets hung on her office wall, one for each client. Since she's also sorted them in chronological order, she can process them by date received. "This way, I always have a backup to see why I processed this first," she says, adding, "but that's never been a problem."

▶ Card 'Em, Dan-o

Patients change and lose jobs, spouses, and dependents with sometimes amazing rapidity. Some patients can change surnames several times in the course of as many years. Any of these alterations can result in a loss of or substantial change in insurance coverage.

Therefore, make sure your clients do the following:

▶ *Card 'em.* Ask to see insurance identification cards for all patients on a routine basis. Many cards contain valuable information such as special telephone numbers or even an explanation of basic coverage in addition to patient ID. It's also helpful to compare the insurance card to the name and address on the patient's drivers' license, so ask for that too.

▶ *Copy it.* Make a photocopy of the insurance card at every appointment and use it to verify the member number and/or group number on the "Patient Registration" form. Insurance ID cards usually carry the effective date of coverage. It's important to note that these cards are frequently issued and distributed to beneficiaries in advance—sometimes as much as 30 days in advance—of the effective date. If the provider renders service prior to the effective date on the card, the patient, not the provider, is responsible for the fee.

▶ *Ask for it.* Obtain job information, including length of employment. Most group plans have a waiting period of at least 30 days and frequently 60 to 90 days before an employee is eligible for coverage.

▶ *Update it.* Unless a doctor is seeing a patient with unusual frequency, the patient should always be asked if there have been any changes in address, phone number, employment, or insurance coverage since the last visit. Have a copy made of his or her driver's license at least once a year—preferably every six months.

▶ *Check it.* Ask Medicaid patients for current proof of eligibility whenever they seek medical care. They are required by federal law to provide it. Eligibility in these programs changes frequently, and benefits will not be paid without adequate proof of eligibility at the time of treatment.

Emailing and faxing are generally viewed as the best ways to go: Information can be sent quickly without worrying about weighing, stamping, or delivery time. The Napa MIB says that 85 percent of their communications is through email. "Doctors love to email," Heidi H. says. "They really don't like to make a lot of calls." Just be sure to install antivirus software on your computer. Also, have a dedicated line so lengthy fax sessions don't tie up your telephone.

The San Diego MIB decided to go with the USPS and provided her doctor with the first quarter's priority mail envelopes and stamps. His staff simply pops a week's worth of day sheets into one of these envelopes, along with any other necessary materials, and consigns it to the postal service.

The personal pickup option works best for the Virginia teacher/MIB. "I'm involved with after-school activities," Kim H. explains, "so I set [aside] Wednesday of every week and I go by each office and pick things up. Then if they have any questions, we take care of it there."

The Walnut Creek MIB also employs the personal pickup option but with a twist. Her beat is the entire San Francisco Bay area, so she uses a courier service. The service picks up from and delivers to her clients' offices every day, five days a week.

In Rockford, Illinois, the former pastor used to drop by his clients' offices once or twice a week, depending on the size of the practice. But now he does everything virtually—either via fax or email.

Organically Organized

Whatever methods you choose, the materials you'll be working with will fall into these basic categories:

- ▶ New patient information sheets and information sheets detailing changes to established patients' files
- ▶ Superbills or day sheets with CPT and ICD-10 codes written in or checked off
- ▶ EOBs for previously submitted claims
- ▶ Mail from insurance carriers and from patients regarding previously submitted claims or changes in policies or patient information

Ideally, all these materials will be presorted for you in chronological order and batched by type of material. You may want to train your clients to present them to you this way, or you may prefer to save them the hassle and sort through it yourself.

If you pick up the material in person, you should take the time to give everything the once-over and make sure you have the information you need. Look, for example, at the superbills or day sheets. Are codes entered or checked? Is the necessary patient information entered and legible? Is it clear whom mail is from or about? Giving all this a glance in your client's office can save you time—you can collect missing information then instead of having to call the client when you return to your office.

warning

Newbie MIBs are sometimes confused about whether they can accept reimbursement checks for the doctor in their company name. The answer is no. Medicare's reassignment laws stipulate that payment must go to the physician, unless he reassigns payment to the facility—an HMO, for example—where he works on-site. As a full-practice management company, you can, however, have checks in the doctor's name come to your office for deposit into his account.

If you're an organically organized person, this extra step in the client's office will be easy for you. If you're easily distracted or flustered, you may find this difficult at first. But take a deep breath, take it easy and train yourself to look things over. Realize that the impression you leave will be one of quiet efficiency.

Once you get back to your own space—or once you receive the material from your friendly mail carrier or fax machine—you'll want to sort through and organize it as we've discussed.

The San Diego MIB/former nurse, who receives her day sheets by mail, makes a habit of emailing requests for corrected coding to her doctor. "They would rather you ask a lot of questions than just decide on your own what you think should happen," she says.

If she feels any information is missing, she dashes off an email request, giving the client the option of calling or emailing back the response. "I do that," she explains, "because I don't want too many verbal requests over the phone, so that I have something to back up that I have requested [the material]."

The Instant "A"

Your software miraculously produces your claims, ready for online delivery, but to where? This is where the clearinghouse comes in. Like a railroad roundhouse sending steaming locomotives to all corners of the country from its central location, the clearinghouse rounds up all your claims and routes them to the proper insurance carriers.

As an added bonus, it reconfigures your data into whatever format each carrier requires, a nice touch because, although the Form CMS 1500 (previously called an HCFA 1500 Form) is the industry standard, insurers still insist on variations on the main theme.

Even better, the clearinghouse automatically *audits* each claim, checking it for clerical errors and omissions before sending it on to the carrier. When it finds a goof, it redirects the claim back to you so you can correct the problem. This way you get an instant "A" with the carrier.

All this may sound alarmingly high-tech, but it's not. If you're the least bit mainstreamed into today's world, you've been using *electronic data interchange*, or EDI, for years. Every time you snatch some cash from the ATM or pass your credit card through the little scanner at the supermarket, you're initiating an EDI transaction.

You may, however, choose not to use a clearinghouse for all your claims. In most areas it's just as easy—and less expensive—to submit directly to Medicare and Blue Cross as it is to send claims through the clearinghouse.

aha!

Set up a system that helps keep the work flowing and the deadlines met. Some MIBs create a computerized spreadsheet; others mark their work on a project board or pencil assignments on a calendar. The key is to come up with a system that works for you so you won't overcommit yourself.

► The Eligibility Factor

During predetermination, the doctor finds out from the insurance carrier the maximum dollar amount it will pay for certain services, procedures, or supplies before he goes ahead and provides them. This is somewhat akin to the good old days when you stood around in the department store while they called your charge card to make sure you had enough balance remaining to cover that gorgeous sequined gown.

Predetermination (also known as coverage or benefits verification) lets both the doctor and the patient know how much of the doctor's charge will be reimbursed by the carrier. It also allows both doctor and patient to make arrangements to cover any difference between the actual charge amount and the allowed amount before service is rendered.

The doctor's office calls the insurance carrier at the phone number listed on the back of the patient's insurance card and explains that they want to verify eligibility. They should then ask the carrier a series of questions, which you can find on the "Predetermination Form," Figure 3–3 on page 61.

You can give copies of this form to your clients as is, or customize it with your business name or your client's. Like the "Precertification Form," this is a great marketing/public relations piece.

Predetermination Form

Patient's name: _____

Date of birth: _____

Subscriber's name: _____

Member no.: _____ Group no.: _____

Insurance carrier: _____

Phone no.: _____

❑ Is there a deductible? _____

If yes, what is it? _____

❑ Has the deductible been met? _____

❑ Is a portion of the intended fee covered under major medical benefits? _____

❑ Is a portion covered under basic benefits? _____

❑ What are the benefits for inpatient care? _____

_____

❑ What are the benefits for outpatient or office care? _____

_____

❑ What percentage of the charge do you reimburse? _____

❑ Is that a percentage of the fee or of usual and customary reimbursement (UCR)? ____

❑ If UCR, can you give me a rough estimate of your reimbursement for our charge of

$_____ for a _____ (code)? $_____

❑ Is there an annual maximum? _____

❑ If yes, how much has been used? _____

FIGURE 3–3: **Predetermination Form**

Clearinghouses generally charge a processing fee, which ranges from 20 cents to 95 cents per claim. Some charge an annual registration or membership fee of up to $300; others add a one-time fee of to $50 to $100 per doctor. (We'll go over all this in depth in Chapter 6.)

The Old-Fashioned Way

Electronic claims transmission is the recommended method of submitting insurance claims, but not everyone is on board yet. A few insurers still accept only paper claims, and some MIBs prefer dealing with paper claims.

"We do not do electronic filing of claims," says the Denver MIB, "as we've had very bad luck finding a clearinghouse that would efficiently handle physicians' claims and do it correctly."

New clients are surprised when she tells them she does only paper claims, especially since the other billing services in her area all file electronically, but she manages to reassure them. "I get payment back within two to three weeks on most all my claims," she asserts, "even though I send them through the U.S. Postal Service."

Another joy of running your own billing service: You can use any system that works for you.

Submission Time

After you've entered the day's claims, it's time for the big moment—submitting them. If you're working with paper claims, you print them out—one copy for your files and one for the insurer—and set your copy aside. Then it's just a matter of fold, lick, and stamp.

If you're working with electronic claims, you'll go to the online portion of your software and send the day's batch speeding to your clearinghouse or carrier. Some clearinghouses will *drop the claims to paper* for you, meaning you send the claim online and the clearinghouse prints a paper copy and sends it on its merry way.

> **tip** ⓘ
>
> File claims as quickly and frequently as possible, once a week at the very least. Remember, the faster you get claims to the carrier, the faster your client will get paid.

By the time you've scooted to the kitchen for a fresh cup of coffee, the clearinghouse will have received your claims, forwarded the good, or clean, copies to the respective carriers, and alerted you to the rejected ones—if any—via a report called the *Audit/Error Report* or *Sender Log*.

At this point you can and should print the report for your records. You can also make corrections to the rejects and resubmit. In the case of rejects (such as incorrect codes) that need doctor clarification, you can call the client immediately or set the claim aside to be dealt with later.

Playing the Insurance Game

A given in the medical billing industry is that insurers will thwart you at every turn with an apparently insatiable desire to deny claims. They seem to find every possible reason to reject a claim or to avoid prompt payment. The savvy MIB takes on the challenge instead of being oppressed by it.

"You learn how to play with the insurance companies," counsels Mary V., the Maryland MIB. "We have to view it as a game. I look at it as somebody's got to win. And I don't like to lose."

Mary advises not taking the game personally and offers the fact that, with her philosophy, she doesn't get a lot of rejections. "Because if you learn the game," she says, "if you learn what they're looking for, then they'll pay."

As an example, Mary cites an HMO that rejects a paper claim because the referral wasn't attached, even though it was fastened with three staples. "You just send it back in as quickly as possible," she says. She speeds the EOB or denial back through with not only a copy of the referral attached but the referral number, the date, and her initials inked on the front. "And they don't reject that one."

Mary cheerfully explains that it's also possible to intimidate the insurance carrier. "You do it nicely," she says. "But they know that you're not going to give up. It's basically if they know you're serious about what you're talking about—you're going to call them back— then they will go on and pay it."

The Walnut Creek, California, MIB also cites HMOs as difficult adversaries. "Trying to get timely payments is sometimes very difficult even if you electronically bill," she says. "They know all of the ways not to pay you. They will send our patient, for instance, a letter requesting further information, and the patient presumes the billing is being handled and frequently ignores their letter, so they don't have to respond until the patient responds. So it's a cat-and-mouse game."

The New Jersey MIB, who used to sit on the insurer side of the fence, adds with a touch of whimsy, "I used to fight on behalf of the insurance companies, and now I fight with them."

In Illinois, Curt J. has experienced the biller/carrier relationship quite differently. "Actually," he says, "that part of [the gamesmanship] surprised me. Most of the time it's really straightforward. It's either an error, a glitch, or a communication problem. Sometimes it can take a little bit to figure out, but once it's figured out, it's done. There's actually very few of the games that you hear insurance companies play."

Back in Virginia, Kim H., the teacher, finds that interactions with insurers don't always go quite so smoothly. When she sees a denial on an EOB, she reaches for the phone and calls the carrier. "You wouldn't believe that you could be on hold for ten minutes just to check out one claim," she says ruefully. "When I get through, they tell me what the problem is, so I immediately try to take care of it. And then I just rebill it."

▶ The Rejected Claim

Face it. No matter how brilliant you are, you're going to have some rejected claims. Sometimes it's because the insurance company is playing fast and loose; sometimes it's because somebody left out vital information.

The following are common reasons for rejected claims:

- ▶ Missing or incomplete diagnosis
- ▶ Missing or incorrect subscriber and/or group number
- ▶ Diagnosis does not correspond with or support the services or procedures performed
- ▶ Diagnosis is not ICD-10 coded
- ▶ Reasons for multiple visits made the same day are not given
- ▶ Charges are not itemized
- ▶ Fee column is left blank
- ▶ Required information about prescription drugs or durable medical equipment is not included
- ▶ Missing or incorrect CPT codes
- ▶ Patient did not answer all questions on his portion of form
- ▶ Incorrect dates—for example, surgery shown taking place before pre-op exam, or discharge date preceding admission date
- ▶ Missing dates
- ▶ Illegible claim—smeary, smudged, handwritten in a scrawl, coffee-spill blurred
- ▶ Service or procedure not covered by policy

Since she's in school until midafternoon, her time is at a premium. "It's hard," Kim admits. "A lot of times if I have quite a few [denials], I'll take the planning period that I have at school, which is about 45 minutes, and I'll call during that time. A lot of times I have to come straight home and then from 3:30 to 5:00 I try to call."

Winning the Game

It should be obvious by now that to be a savvy MIB, you have to be willing to play, and play to win. You can't be a wimp.

If you have not received payment on a claim within 45 days after submission, it's time to find out what the problem is.

> **tip** ⓘ
>
> Most insurers have an 800 number. Be sure you use it, so your on-hold time is on their quarter instead of yours. If the phone number you have is not toll free, ask for one when you get a live being on the line; frequently, they'll give you one for future reference. (Or hang up and call back on the 800 number.)

Sometimes it's simply a matter of nonreceipt. The claim may have been lost in the mail, sucked into an alternate universe, or mysteriously vaporized within the carrier's computer system.

Some carriers require written inquiries; some Medicare and Medicaid carriers require specific inquiry forms; some carriers allow telephone inquiries. In any case, you should copy all written inquiries and annotate them to the patient file. For telephone questions, be sure to get the name and phone extension of the person you speak with and note these details on your file along with the date and particulars of the conversation. If it's apparent the payer has made an error on a claim, don't hesitate to challenge the payment amount. Medicare and other insurers will correct mistakes if you bring them to their attention. Even if you made the error, it's always possible to resubmit a claim.

When you discover an error on a claim that has resulted in insufficient reimbursement, submit a corrected claim. Clearly mark the claim: *Corrected Billing—Not a Duplicate Claim.* Add a note specifying the error and, if necessary, additional documentation to support your correction.

Don't think your entire MIB life will be spent battling insurers. Most of the claims you submit will be paid quickly, allowing you to post the payment to the patient's account and bill the patient for any co-payment due.

When you do encounter the odd problem claim, however, you'll be armed and ready. You already know the secret: Be prepared to fix and/or fight.

When you receive a patient's EOB (explanation of benefits), start grading the insurer's work. Compare the charge amount listed with the charge amount in your patient's account ledger.

Check your client's codes against those on the EOB for errors or changes that the carrier might have made. Sometimes payers will down-code a procedure from the actual one to a less costly one—inadvertently or intentionally—and pay based on the substituted code. In

▶ Faster Than a Speeding Bullet

As a mega-MIB, your goal is to get claims paid as quickly as possible. You can't leap tall buildings in a single bound (at least we don't think you can), but you can get claims reimbursed at seemingly super speeds. Try these tips for starters:

▶ *Rank procedures by order of charge amount.* When entering charges, be sure to enter all procedures performed on the same date in order, from the most expensive to the least expensive. Insurers will reduce the values of all procedures listed after the primary one. If you list the procedures as suggested, however, your claim will result in the highest possible reimbursement in light of the carrier's reduction of values. You should always list the full charge for each procedure and let the carrier reduce them—don't help them out. In most cases, the first procedure is considered at 100 percent of its value, the second at 75 percent, the third at 50 percent, and the fourth at 25 percent.

▶ *Don't send documentation unless asked.* Although electronic claims don't require documentation, people tend to send documentation along with paper claims. Don't. Unless the provider is using a CPT code for an unlisted procedure or explaining unusual circumstances (unsticking a patient's eyelids after a superglue accident, for example), you should not send operative reports or other documentation. Most procedures are fairly common, so carriers won't even be interested in the details. If they want supporting information, they'll ask. Otherwise, let sleeping insurers lie.

▶ *Send even hospital bills frequently.* Carriers prefer to get frequent, small claims instead of one huge claim following the patient's discharge. While some providers hold hospital charges as a consideration to the hospitalized patient, you can help avoid a tragic relapse caused by a mammoth doctor's fee simply by doing your billing as you—and the patient's care—go along. Also, holding claims through a long hospitalization is risky. You could discover that by the time you get around to filing your claim, the patient's benefits have already been exhausted.

some cases, the payer's data entry department may simply have transposed two digits in a CPT code, resulting in a different procedure from the one performed. In other cases, your client might have used an outdated CPT code that the insurer did not—or refused to—recognize. Here the insurer may review the claim and pop in the valid code for you or deny the claim and leave it up to you to resubmit.

tip

If you're not getting a response from a recalcitrant carrier, use your patient as a collection tool. Inform him of the problem and let him go toe-to-toe with the insurer. In many cases, this will result in a quick resolution of the problem.

Time Juggling

Except for having to work within the time constraints of the carriers' office hours when dealing with problem claims, you can structure your day any way that fits your lifestyle.

"I just work into the evening if I need to have the extra time," says a Montana MIB. As a grandmom rather than young mom, she has the luxury of time. "I'll just juggle my time, and I don't have to worry that I have an eight-to-five job. I can do the work that needs to be completed in my time frame."

The San Diego biller has her hands full with two school-aged children. Before the kids are up and about, she checks her email for new information from fellow MIBs, then pulls up her prospect software to see who she has scheduled to contact that day. In between getting her chicks fed, dressed, and off to school, she compiles lists: which insurance companies need to be called, what missing items need to be faxed to her client.

To avoid the unprofessional sound of children squealing in the background, she makes all her phone calls in the morning while the kids are at school. She schedules errands between noon and 2 P.M. when most medical offices are closed so she doesn't miss business calls. In the afternoons, she does her data entry, pulls up reports, balances her accounts, and checks through new material, and of course, answers the phone.

"Then," the former nurse says, "I sort of semi-prepare myself for the next day. By the end of the day, I back up my database for my client. And then every week, I'll do a system backup."

Lest you think you could never keep up her pace, she adds, "I'm still in the learning stages. I'm constantly adapting to what I'm doing, and sometimes I worry that I spend too much time on something. But it's all a learning process."

The New Jersey MIB, who also has two young children, usually processes her claims from 12:30 to 4:00 P.M. while the kids are stashed away at school. After supper, she goes back to her computer and hits the keyboard again. She schedules two days a week, generally Thursday and Friday, for follow-up work. "That's for any problems that come up with the clients," she says, "if I have to call the insurance company, do an appeal, things like that."

And that's not all. "I'm often working Saturdays," she says. "I refuse to work on Sunday, though. No matter what."

Diagnosing Your Market

E very business needs consumers for its products or services to, as the Vulcans so eloquently put it, live long and prosper. Now that you know what running a medical billing service entails, you need to diagnose, or target, your market to determine who your potential clients will be, what geographic area you'll draw from, and what specific services you'll offer to lure them in.

This is an important phase in the mega-MIB building project. The proper market research can help boost your billing service into a true profit center, and the more research you do, the better prepared you'll be before you officially open your doors, and the less floundering you are likely to do. This chapter, therefore, homes in on market research tips and techniques for the budding medical billing service. We'll cover a lot of ground in this chapter, so to help you stay focused and organized, we have provided a "Market Research Checklist," Figure 4–3, on page 84.

Tripping Doctors

Your target market—the clients you are aiming for—can be as wide as the field of modern medicine. Any health-care provider is fair game. You can go after family practitioners, providers of every specialty from geriatrics to pediatrics, chiropractors and osteopaths, obstetricians and oncologists, proctologists and podiatrists. You can target mental health

► On a Mission

The mission statement is an important part of brainstorming any new business. This is where you state your company's intent or goals and what you'll do to achieve them. You might choose something like:

Acme Billing Service will provide full-practice management to neurologists and urologists, offering quality billing, patient accounting, and tips and updates on the latest collection techniques. Through the speed and efficiency of our collections, we will become recognized as the premier neurology and urology billing service in Huckleberry, New Hampshire. We will have a ten-physician base within two years.

Here's another example:

Zephyr Claims Services will provide the best and brightest in claims billing for nursing homes and hospices. Because of our expertise with Medicare and our ability to get claims reimbursed quickly, we will sign five clients in our first year of operation and will have 20 by the end of our second year.

Like everything else we've covered in this chapter, what you choose to say and how you say it is up to you. See Figure 4–1 on page 71 for a worksheet to help you craft a mission statement as unique and personal as you are.

Mission Statement Worksheet

Fill in your mission statement on this worksheet. Remember that the mission statement should clearly define the following:

▶ *A view to the future.* How do you envision your business down the road, in one year, two years, ten years?

▶ *A view to your clients' perception of your company.* How do you want them to think of you?

▶ *A view to the medical community at large.* How do you wish the medical community to perceive your company?

Mission Statement for

_____

(your business name)

_____

_____

_____

_____

_____

_____

_____

_____

_____

_____

_____

FIGURE 4–1: **Mission Statement Worksheet**

professionals, psychiatrists, and psychologists. And don't forget the groups of providers not normally associated with doctoring, such as dentists, social workers, nursing homes, ambulance services, pharmacists, home health practitioners, providers of durable medical equipment, and providers of bionic body parts. The only essential requirement is that they bill or receive reimbursement from insurance carriers or patients.

This doesn't mean, however, that your best technique is to stand at the hospital doors, tripping doctors as they walk by. Targeting by definition means homing in on a particular group.

If you have had previous experience working in a particular medical specialty, for example, you might want to target that market first. You'll feel comfortable with the jargon and procedures so your sales pitch—and your initial billings—will go smoother and easier. As an added bonus, you may already have contacts in the field who can either become your first clients or steer you on to colleagues in the field.

If you're a newbie in the world of medicine, you might want to start off targeting doctors in a single specialty, such as psychiatrists, chiropractors, cardiologists, or dentists. These providers' practices involve a narrower range of diagnoses and procedures than a family practitioner, general surgeon, or internist, so you'll have fewer new codes tossed in your lap at the get-go.

This is a good, starting-from-scratch strategy, but don't let it dictate or limit your contacts. Most MIBs find that the first client they land, through whatever means, is the specialty they end up going with.

Curt J.'s client base originally consisted of one dentist and two chiropractors. The dentist was easy—he's a personal friend. Of the chiropractors, the first was a case of serendipity.

"I ran across a struggling chiropractic office," the Illinois MIB relates. "They just needed help, so I began to help them. Shortly after we began building a relationship, they filed for bankruptcy. But it was enough of a foot in the door that they had a couple of friends that they recommended to me, and that helped me land a couple of accounts."

The New Jersey MIB's clients are all mental health professionals. Of 26 individual providers, every one is a psychiatrist, psychologist, or biofeedback technician. Surprisingly, however, she did not actively go after the mental health field. "It just sort of found me," she says. "Once I got my first client—who was actually given to me—it rolled from there by word of mouth and referrals."

The nub of these experiences—that the first client helps to land others—is a familiar one. We heard over and over from just about everyone we have spoken with in the MIB trade that doctors talk. When one likes what you are doing, he will tell another and she will tell another. Next thing you know, you will be knee-deep in doctors.

"Just by default, my first client was a neurologist," the Denver MIB says. "I haven't really marketed my services; it's been by word of mouth." Her stable of clients is 14 strong—13 neurologists and one family physician. "That's not by choice; it just happened that way. I guess my name has been passed around in the neurology locker room."

Mary V. originally specialized in neurology as well as oncology. She felt she was better off sticking to the fields she enjoys, ones in which she is familiar with the coding. She's also wisely figured that by specializing, she'll be less affected by regulatory changes than if they had a broader client base. "When something happens with one specialty," Mary explains, "then it would

> **fun fact** ☺
>
> A new study by the American Medical Association shows that the majority of American physicians (60.7 percent) still work in small practices of ten or few doctors. This is good news for MIBs who want to focus on a particular niche or specialty.

happen for all of [the doctors] as far as changes in any rule or code or something like that. It is just much quicker, much easier to follow up on. My staff and I don't have to be experts in everything."

On the flip side, the Napa MIB is open to all specialties. "One of the things I never wanted to do was put myself in a box," says Heidi H. "Even my school mentor told me to pick a specialty and stick with it and build your business around that one specialty. But I didn't think it was a good idea to put myself in that box. So, I do any and all specialties that come to me." Apparently, this has been a successful strategy as her business has grown to include six employees over the last few years.

Keep in mind that not all referrals need to come from doctors. In an interesting twist, Sandra S. from Minnesota, has connected with a medical attorney who refers her services to doctors he works with.

Does Size Really Matter?

OK, you've decided—or you are thinking about planning on deciding—which areas to specialize in. Good! But you are far from laying your decision-making skills to rest. Next, you have to think about what size practices you will want to focus on. Any size is fine, of course, but you might consider starting off with small to midsize practices. This way, you won't be overwhelmed by your workload while you are on the upside of your learning curve.

You should also consider the size to which you want your practice ultimately to grow. "If you don't want to be big, you don't want to grow a whole lot," Mary V. counsels. "[Then] you want three or four doctors. That's going to give you a very good income, depending on the type of doctor you have."

"We love our chiropractor," Mary adds as an example, "but I will never take on another one."

Why? "Sheer volume," Mary says. "A chiropractor can see a hundred patients a day in one fell swoop, and you've got all this paper here, whereas a neurologist sees 20 to 26 [patients per day]."

Even though both doctors bring in the same amount of money for a day's work, Mary explains, the chiropractor, billing at $45 per visit, must generate far more claims—and more work for the MIB—than the neurologist, who's billing $100 and up per visit.

What's My Niche?

OK, you've narrowed down which specialties you'll target. Now you'll want to find your niche, the unique angle that will set your business apart from—and above—the competition. This is where you can really let your creativity shine through.

Mary V. once marketed holistic health products such as vitamins and minerals along with her billing services. "What we found," she explains, "is that we are marrying that into our billing service. Both feed off the other. We were going to see this doctor's wife who called us three times since she heard about it. She wanted to get into it because he's a neurologist; he sees that this could help his patients."

► Portrait of a Client

Medical billing clients come from every spectrum of every specialty. They can be retirees on their way out or handsome young hunks on their way up. Large practices contract with MIBs as often as small ones. Medical billing clients are sophisticated big-city types and small-town trenchers, HMO employees, and the self-employed.

The typical client is, however, more likely to be a doctor than a dentist, and far more likely to be a doctor than an ambulance service. However, that shouldn't stop you from pursuing a pharmacy, home health practitioner, nursing home, assisted living facility, or durable medical goods provider.

Other than these basics, the portrait of a typical medical billing client is delightfully blank. You can fill in just about any provider you care to go after.

Another service she offers their clients is recommendations to strengthen the business. "I had been seeing this oncologist's income just going down," the former customer service tech relates, "and I [thought] 'Well, she's billing out more. Why is her income going down?'"

Mary ran a comparison of the doctor's income between the previous and current years and determined that although the woman was billing a fair amount of money in chemotherapy drugs, she wasn't doing the amount of consultations necessary to bring in income.

"We went in with a bunch of recommendations as to what she needs to do to get that money back up," Mary explains. "We're going to set up a bunch of things to get her networking, to get her consults back up. That's how she's going to survive. She's not going to survive on drugs alone; there's just no markup there."

Starting from Retiring

The New Jersey MIB started her business closing down other people's businesses. A family friend, who also happened to be a pediatrician, asked her to take over his billing temporarily until he could find a replacement for the office manager who had just quit. She took on the task in addition to her full-time job with the health insurance carrier.

"And then he informed me that he was going to retire in a year and he really didn't want to go through the hassle of hiring and training somebody," she says. "He asked, 'Would I like to finish up before he retired?' I said, 'Oh, what the heck.' Extra money, you know. Next thing I know, a few months later he says, 'I have this friend who lives in my development; he's a chiropractor and he really could use somebody.'"

It turned out that the chiropractor was getting ready for retirement, too, so Linda took on his billing and got him cleaned up to retire. "And I said, 'What the heck, this would be a good business to start on my own.'"

The focus of her business has changed; she now bills for mental health providers who are not retiring. But the niche she started from is an excellent example of finding a unique angle. You might want to concentrate

> **tip** ⓘ
>
> The folks at Optum360 publish a couple of books, the *Customized Fee Analyzer* and the *National Fee Analyzer*, that show you what physicians are currently charging and what insurers are paying, as well as provide data for negotiating favorable managed care contracts. They will even customize the charge rates for your zip code area. Check out www.optum360coding. com for all their products.

on "cleaning up" retiring providers or on gearing up brand-new doctors who can't yet afford an in-house staff.

You might consider specializing in far-flung providers, those who live and work in remote, rural areas where there are no billing services. Or how about making personal service your niche? You can offer to handle your clients' noninsured patient billing as well so that you cover the full spectrum of charges and payments.

"Use your background," Mary V. suggests. "What did you do? What can you offer the office? That's really what got us thinking [about] what else we could offer."

Go the Extra Mile

You can go the extra mile, offering additional services for which, of course, you'll ask an additional fee. But at the same time, you'll be tailoring your services and making yourself and your business indispensable. Here are some ideas to kick-start your own creativity:

▶ *Management reports.* Give your clients up-to-the-nanosecond reports on everything that affects their productivity and income. Punch out charts and graphs on all kinds of interesting stuff: how often the doctor performs a specific procedure in a given time period; how many patients she sees on a daily, weekly, or monthly basis; how much of her business is accounted for by various insurance companies. This sort of information can be very helpful as the doctor negotiates contracts with insurers and HMOs and can be a major selling point for your service.

▶ *Account collections.* Put the squeeze on insurance carriers and patients for unpaid claims and bills.

▶ *Fee analysis.* Review your clients' fee schedules. Compare them with the reasonable and customary fees for their area and the current Medicare schedule. Suggest adjustments.

> **tip** ⓘ
>
> After the interview, always send a short thank-you note. This is not only simple courtesy, but it also sets a nice tone for future relations. Handle your telephone interviews the same way. Ask ahead, be professional, and follow up with a thank you.

▶ *Secondary claims.* Send secondary claims—for example, claims in which a husband and wife are supplementally covered by each other's employer's group insurance—after the primary has paid its portion.

▶ *Patient statements.* Print and mail monthly statements to cash and co-payment patients. As another service, you can post them, too.

▶ *Patient birthdays.* Print out a monthly or quarterly list of upcoming big days so the doctor's office can send cards. Or send the cards yourself on behalf of the doctor's office.

▶ *Medical transcription.* Type up reports and chart notes or even medical research papers. Medical transcription is usually a service in itself and requires special training, but you can use subcontractors and offer it as a part of your package.

Up Close and Personal

Along with targeting your market—determining in which specialty you're going to start— you'll want to begin your market research.

Personal interviews are an excellent way to do this. Be sure you call first to schedule a short meeting at a time convenient to your interviewee. It's professional courtesy to presume (correctly) that other people have busy schedules. Let your subject know the reason for the interview and about how much of his or her time you expect to take, and possibly even divulge a few of the questions you'll be asking. This will put them at ease about the interview and also get them thinking ahead.

"Before I bought [my software package]," Kim H. says, "I went to our hospital administrator and to people in the area and talked to them to see if there was a need because I really wasn't familiar with the medical billing myself."

Not only did Kim discover the real need for medical billing in her area—she also made a valuable contact. "The hospital administrator [referred] me to other doctors who were moving into the area," she explains. "So I really didn't have to spend a lot of money to market myself; I was really fortunate in that aspect."

Ready, Willing, and Able

Besides going out and talking to people face to face, you can conduct a direct-mail survey. This serves a dual purpose: It's another way to explore your potential market, and it's a great marketing tool. While you're asking questions, you can let your future clients know that you're ready, willing, and able to take care of them.

"My initial contact with most of my contacts has been through an insurance-processing-claims survey," the San Diego MIB says. "I've been getting a lot of responses from chiropractors, although my target market initially was health-care providers that weren't filing electronically to Medicare."

aha!

Surf the web for online market research. You'll find everything from medical billers to physicians' account management specialists to the American Medical Association.

fun fact   ☺

The Geezer states (ones with the highest numbers of Medicare enrollees) are California, Florida, New York, Texas, and Pennsylvania, according to CMS.

Check with your local Medicare carrier for a list of doctors who are not filing electronically. "It came on a disc," she explains, "and all I did was just copy and paste it into my word-processing program and print it up!"

Put some creativity into your surveys. You want to appear professional but at the same time informative and entertaining. Your respondents are more apt to answer a direct-mail piece that catches their attention than a poorly written one that drags. Keep your survey short and sweet. You can offer two options: a fax number for fax-return responses and a SASE (self-addressed stamped envelope) for mail-back responses.

The Economic Pulse

While you're checking out potential clients, you can start on your next task: taking your region's economic pulse.

Economically depressed areas do not generate many health-care provider visits, except perhaps for Medicaid ones, and these, as you know, are not the most highly paid. If an area shows evidence of hard times, chances are people are not spending money on doctor visits. Hence, the local medics are not going to have a lot of work for you.

If, on the other hand, the neighbors are the Range-Rover-in-every-driveway type, then you can rest assured that they're health conscious and willing and able to spend the money necessary to stay healthy. Doctors in this neighborhood will have plenty of claims to bill.

Is your neighborhood—or one that you'd like to target—largely dependent on a nearby military base? If so, then you need to research how many of its residents get their health care free of charge at the base hospital and how many use TRICARE. The easiest way to do this is to call local physicians and get a ballpark estimate of how many TRICARE patients or families they serve.

If the neighborhood is dependent on a large industrial concern such as an auto assembly plant, then you can ascertain how many of its residents are covered by union or plant health insurance. How? Ask workers, ask neighbors, ask doctors. Call the plant's human resources department and ask them. If the plant is up and running and financially healthy, you can figure that

aha!

Contact your local chamber of commerce or city hall for information on local demographics. Often, this data is available online. Your local library may also be a useful source of information.

health-care dollars will be spent. But you also need to consider—again by asking around and by reading local newspapers—whether the plant is in any danger of shutting down. A neighborhood where a large portion of the population is suddenly unemployed is not going to bode well for doctor dollars.

stat fact

According to the CMS, total health spending is estimated to reach $3.2 trillion this year, which averages out to $10,000 spent on each person.

You can examine your neighborhood, town, or county under the same magnifying glass, but instead of looking at the military and heavy-industry sector, check into the white-collar core. In an area like Burbank, California, for example, peopled with movie studios from Warner Bros. to Disney, a large percentage of the population has union connections and hence health-care insurance. In Erie, Pennsylvania, everybody seems to work for GE Transportation. Well, you get the picture.

The Wonderful World of Wifi

One of the really exciting options in the MIB trade is that your business doesn't have to be restricted to your own neighborhood. Between mail, fax, and the internet, you can serve just about any client anywhere.

▶ Direct-Mail Dazzle

Because of the ability to target well-defined geographical areas, direct mail can be an effective way to promote your medical claims billing service. It also allows you to send a personalized sales message.

There is no magic formula when using direct mail, except that using a solo mailer is more successful than including your information in a cooperative mailer full of supermarket coupons. You can send a flashy postcard, informative brochure, or a sales letter with a personal touch (see the letter example in Figure 10–1, on page 159).

Statistically, a 1 percent direct-mail response rate is considered excellent, so if you mail 1,000 pieces and receive ten phone calls, that's a great turnaround. Mailing lists can be purchased from list brokers, which you can find online under "Advertising—Direct Mail." These lists come in just about every category, and since you've done your marketing homework, you already know the lists you want. Add value to your direct mailer by presenting some sort of bonus offer such as a discount.

Most medical billers serve local providers. They can build a personal relationship based on face-to-face encounters. They can run across the street or across town with material if they feel the need.

But many MIBs are enjoying cross-country relations. The San Diego biller is working on plans to take over the billings of a company based back East. And a member of her networking group, a woman who relocated from Colorado to San Diego, still services her Colorado clients. The Minnesota MIB gets some of her business from a professional freelance site called Upwork (www.upwork.com). This is a good way to virtually build your client base and work with a variety of health providers.

The Competition

A little competition is fine—it shows that there is a market for your services. But like Christmas cookies or New Year's Eve champagne, it's possible to have too much of a good thing. If your area is already swamped with medical billing services, you'll need to brainstorm a way to make your service different—and more appealing—than everyone else's. Of the MIBs across the country who interviewed for this book, however, this was never a problem, so don't panic. The field is big enough that there seems to be plenty of room for everyone who's serious about the job.

Still, you are going to face some competition, and it's going to come from two primary sources: in-house billing clerks and other medical billing services.

The best way to compete with in-house billing is to find out as much as possible about how the typical doctor's office operates and then formulate a competitive strategy. Check out, for example, how many other responsibilities the in-house biller has. Frequently, she's also the receptionist/secretary and is signing in patients, making appointments, answering phones, and making or receiving referrals at the same time as she's handling insurance and patient billing. She's going in so many directions at once that she has little or no time to follow up on unpaid claims and no incentive to streamline, update, or expand the system.

Your marketing strategy for dealing with this type of competition is simple: You'll devote all your time to claims processing, follow-up, and billing, leaving to the office staff the important work of dealing with patients.

Nosy—Not!

Some people blanch at the thought of doing the type of research we have just discussed. It's hard enough, they feel, to approach strangers with a bunch of questions. When they factor in asking questions about the very subject they're vitally interested in, they get the small-business version of stage fright.

Don't let this happen to you. There's nothing to be nervous about. You're not being nosy; you're doing research. Plus, here's a secret: Most people love talking about themselves and their jobs. Wouldn't you? It's flattering to have someone take an interest in what you're doing.

Call a couple of medical offices and ask to speak to the person who handles the billing. You can explain exactly why you're calling. Ask if she has a couple of minutes to spare to answer your questions or, if not, find out when a good time to call back would be. Or send in a questionnaire like the one in Figure 4–2 on page 82. Just remember to include a SASE (self-addressed stamped envelope.

You might start with your own doctor's staff. After all, you're their client—you have a pre-existing "in."

Also keep in mind that this is a good opportunity to start marketing your services. Usually, if you're excited about your new business, other people will be, too. Don't be afraid to let your enthusiasm show. Hope for contagion, because at the same time you're seeking information, you'll be making valuable contacts.

You might run across some offices that have a dedicated billing clerk. This is stiffer competition, but it doesn't necessarily slam you out of the ballpark. You, after all, will be charging the doctor based on the amount of money you collect, as opposed to the in-house clerk, who gets paid a set salary whether or not she brings in reimbursements.

Shopping the Competition

As far as competition from outsource billing services, take on the challenge. Think of it as a positive rather than a negative. Here's your chance to see how others are already doing what

▶ Doctor Dialing

Stumped on what to ask in your telephone survey? At a loss for what to wonder? Fear not. Figure 4–4, on page 87, provides a collection of the most up-to-the-minute, topical, helpful questions to put to providers or, more correctly, their office managers or billing clerks. Make a blank copy of the worksheet for each provider you call.

When you call, remember to ask the person if this is a good time to go over a few items; if it's not, ask when a good time to call back would be.

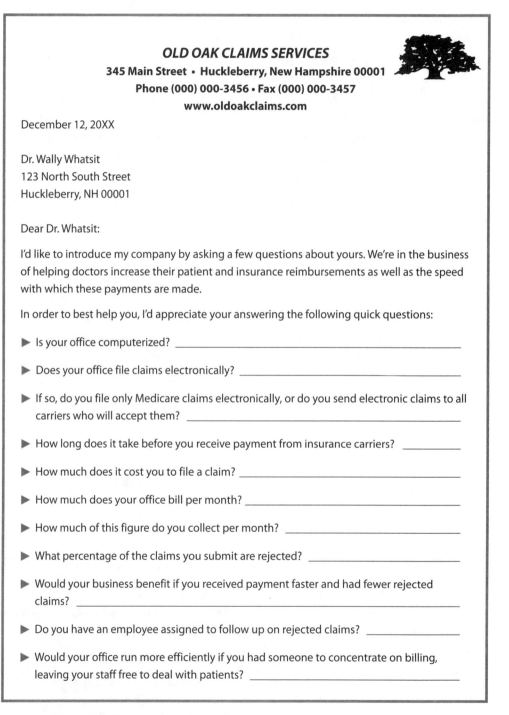

OLD OAK CLAIMS SERVICES
345 Main Street • Huckleberry, New Hampshire 00001
Phone (000) 000-3456 • Fax (000) 000-3457
www.oldoakclaims.com

December 12, 20XX

Dr. Wally Whatsit
123 North South Street
Huckleberry, NH 00001

Dear Dr. Whatsit:

I'd like to introduce my company by asking a few questions about yours. We're in the business of helping doctors increase their patient and insurance reimbursements as well as the speed with which these payments are made.

In order to best help you, I'd appreciate your answering the following quick questions:

▶ Is your office computerized? _____

▶ Does your office file claims electronically? _____

▶ If so, do you file only Medicare claims electronically, or do you send electronic claims to all carriers who will accept them? _____

▶ How long does it take before you receive payment from insurance carriers? _____

▶ How much does it cost you to file a claim? _____

▶ How much does your office bill per month? _____

▶ How much of this figure do you collect per month? _____

▶ What percentage of the claims you submit are rejected? _____

▶ Would your business benefit if you received payment faster and had fewer rejected claims? _____

▶ Do you have an employee assigned to follow up on rejected claims? _____

▶ Would your office run more efficiently if you had someone to concentrate on billing, leaving your staff free to deal with patients? _____

FIGURE 4–2: **Sample Questionnaire**

you plan to do. Shop the competition the same way that you'd shop the mall for a new sweater. Investigate each ad in the same way you'd check out each little boutique. Peer into nooks and crannies by asking lots of questions. Compare competitors' phone personalities, management styles, specialties, and pricing structures the way you'd compare sweater weaves, styles, and prices.

You might discover when you start calling ads from the Yellow Pages that some of your so-called competitors have gone out of business. Others might not be taking on new clients or working in the areas in which you've decided to specialize.

"Actually, all I did," the San Diego MIB says, "was look in the Yellow Pages to see if there were any listings for health-care consultants or billing services. I called them and asked a few questions about [their] pricing so I could get an average of the going rate in my area so I wasn't overpricing or underpricing myself. I asked them how long they were in business and what kind of doctors they were servicing."

She got the information she was after, but not without a few bruised feelings. She learned—as you may, too—that while most people are happy to share information, not everybody is generous.

"Some [billing services] didn't want to talk to me and then actually ended up calling their vendor," the former nurse says. "And then the vendor called me and said that that wasn't an appropriate thing to do.

"This was a vendor I had researched and ended up not going with; I don't know if that had something to do with it. But they said, 'You know, in the business world, that's not really appropriate.' Which I disagree with."

If something like this happens to you, don't take it personally. Some people are easily threatened, taking any hint of competition as a direct hit in the pocketbook or the ego.

> **aha!**
>
> If you're an all-star at underassertiveness and you just know you're going to screw up your approach, try this: Choose a doctor specializing in a field you don't plan to use. Call that office first. Since they're not on your list of "must-have clients," the ones you dread goofing on, your butterfly quotient will drop dramatically. You'll be amazed at how well you do! (And you might even discover you really like that office or specialty and that they're interested in you, too.)

Market Research Checklist

Ready? Hit that target.

❏ Make a list of three markets you'd like to target (e.g., a specialty such as pediatrics or psychiatry, or a particular type of provider such as ambulance services or nursing homes).

1. _____

2. _____

3. _____

❏ Using a copy of the "Providers Survey" in Figure 4–4, page 87 for each business you plan to contact, make your calls and fill in the worksheets. Don't be shy. Call as many providers as possible.

❏ Use the direct mail piece in Figure 4–2, page 82 as a template. (You'll want to put it on your own letterhead.) Send it to as many providers as possible.

❏ Follow up phone calls and returned surveys with thank-you notes.

❏ Schedule interviews with providers, MIBs, or others in your community such as local hospital administrators.

❏ Bring a copy of your survey to use in your interviews.

❏ Follow up interviews with thank yous!

Steady? Correlate your findings.

❏ Correlate your provider information.

Do most providers in your area already outsource their billing? _____

Are most offices computerized? _____

Do most file electronic claims? _____

Of these, do most file only Medicare claims electronically? Or to all accepting carriers?

_____

How long does it take for most providers to receive payment from insurers? _____

How much does it cost most providers to file a claim? _____

FIGURE 4–3: **Market Research Checklist**

Don't be befuddled by market research tasks. Use this handy checklist to coordinate and organize your efforts.

Market Research Checklist

What is the average monthly billable? _____

What is the average monthly collectable? _____

What percentage of claims are rejected? _____

Do most feel their businesses would benefit from your type of service? _____

How many have in-house clerks who do billing and nothing else? _____

How many seem interested in your new service? _____ _

❏ Correlate your billing service information.

What is an average number of clients? _____

What seem to be the most popular specialties? _____

_____

What is the average number of years in operation? _____

What is the average time to get off the ground? _____

What is the overall feeling about competition? _____

_____

What is the average pricing structure? _____ $ _____ per claim

_____ _____ percent

_____ $ _____ per hour

Do most have employees? If yes, how many? _____

If so, what is the pay rate? _____

Averages of answers to your additional questions: _____

Go! Get demographics.

❏ Find out everything you can about the neighborhood, town, or county in which you
wish to operate.

❏ Check with your local chamber of commerce or library.

FIGURE 4–3: **Market Research Checklist,** continued

Market Research Checklist

❑ Get on the internet.

❑ Read local papers.

❑ Talk to your neighbors.

❑ Check with human resources or insurance departments of local large employers.

Keep going! Choose a niche.

❑ Choose three unique angles to make your business shine.

1. _____
_____
_____

2. _____
_____
_____

3. _____
_____
_____

FIGURE 4–3: **Market Research Checklist,** continued

Providers Survey

Provider's business name: _____

Name and title of person giving information: _____

Phone number: _____

❑ Does your office have an outsource billing service? If so, which one and why did you choose it? _____

_____

❑ If not, does your office file claims electronically? _____

❑ If so, do you file only Medicare claims electronically, or do you send electronic claims to all carriers who will accept them? _____

❑ How long does it usually take before you receive payment from insurers? _____

_____

❑ Is your office computerized? _____

❑ Would your business benefit if you received payment faster and had fewer rejected claims? _____

❑ How much does your office bill per month? _____

❑ How much does your office collect per month? _____

❑ What percentage of the claims you submit are rejected? Do you have an employee assigned to follow up on rejected claims? _____

❑ Would your office run more efficiently if you had someone to concentrate on billing, leaving your staff free to deal with patients? _____

❑ Additional questions _____

_____

_____

FIGURE 4–4: **Providers Survey**

Providers Survey

Evaluation

Now, do a personal evaluation:

❏ Was the staffer you spoke with friendly? Could you ask her for advice or suggestions in the future? _____

_____

❏ Was her information in line with similar specialty providers in your area? If not, why not? _____

_____

❏ Did she provide any good tips? If so, what were they? _____

_____

_____

❏ Were you pleased with the interview? Did you feel you handled yourself well? If not, what could you do differently with the next call? _____

_____

_____

❏ Did you remember to follow up with a thank-you note?

FIGURE 4–4: **Providers Survey,** continued

X-Ray of a Medical Billing Business

This chapter could also be called "The Bare Bones" because this is where we delve into the structure of your business from company name to legal form to permits.

Name That Business

Every business, like every child, has to have a name, and you should devote just as much thought to it. After all, you plan to have your business baby around for a long time. You want a name you can be proud of, one that identifies it—and by extension you—as worthy of your clients' confidence.

Because medical billing is a more serious-minded business than, say, pizza delivery or greeting card design, that sobriety should be reflected in your company name. This means, unfortunately for the more frivolous among us, that you can rule out names like Piglet's Claims Processing or Wild for Reimbursements.

Instead, your name should call attention to your expertise and efficiency. The terminally creative, however, can take heart. Businesslike doesn't mean dull. Your name can—and should—deliver a snappy punch.

One MIB calls her company At Your Service. "It starts with an 'A,'" she says, "which gives me a good spot in the Yellow Pages. That's my philosophy for my business. When I present myself to a physician, it's not 'These are my services and you can choose from selection A, B, or C.' It's 'What do you need to run more efficiently in your office now, and how can I be an extension to your office? How can I fill in those gaps and spaces to help your staff run more efficiently and help your whole practice be what it should be?'"

▶ Of Surf and Scoping a Name

You have a terrific source for coming up with a business name right in your own home, probably next to the phone or buried in a drawer. It's your local Yellow Pages! Take a visual trip through the big yellow book, not just in the billing services section but in any other section that strikes your fancy. (How about advertising, architects, or boutiques?)

Do any business names conjure up an image that appeals to you? Identify that image and something similar for your business name. For example, if you see Surfside Interiors, you might consider calling yourself Surf Side Billing Services. Or how about "Bingo Billing Services: You've Hit the Jackpot!" Just kidding.

Though naming your company is without a doubt a creative (and fun) process, it helps to take a systematic approach. Once you've decided on a name, or perhaps two or three possibilities, check to see if any other business has a similar name. Look on the internet, as well as in those handy-dandy Yellow Pages. This will save you time and effort before you file for your fictitious business name.

You want your name to be truly different, to stand out from the crowd and excel, just as your business will.

Buffalo Bill(ing)

Many MIBs incorporate the name of their town or region into their business name. You might consider something like Claims Processors of Chesterfield or Billing Services of Buffalo, or you might want to incorporate a geographic or historical feature of your area, such as Seaside Services if you live at the beach or Alamo Billing and Claims if you live in San Antonio.

Whatever you go with, remember that you'll be repeating your name every time you answer the phone. Sound out the moniker before you settle on it. Some names look great in print but are difficult, if not impossible, to understand over the phone. M & A Associates, for example, may seem like a keen name for partners Marty and Andrea, but when spoken it sounds like MNA. Don't forget that most callers rate about a C-minus in listening comprehension. No matter how clearly you enunciate, they're not going to understand M & A. So save yourself hours of telephone frustration and choose something simple.

For some really good name ideas, check out billing services on the internet. You will want to make yours as individual as you are, but some of those will help start your creative gears turning. Use the "Business Name Brainstorming" worksheet in Figure 5–1, page 92, to help you find one that's right for you.

The Fictitious Business Name

After you've decided on a name, you'll need to register it. Basically, registering your fictitious business name means that you check with the proper authorities to find out if someone else has already appropriated the name you want and then, assuming they haven't, pay a fee to register it as your own. If the name is already in use, you'll need to choose something different, of course. Note that most states do not require you to register a fictitious name or DBA (doing business as) if you are using your own name.

This process varies in different regions of the country. In Florida, for example, you can register your business name online for $50. Once you have certified that you've advertised your fictitious name or DBA for one week, you will receive a certificate listing your name on a nice, official-looking certificate suitable for framing.

In other areas of the country, you might simply pop down to your city or county clerk's office, thumb through the roster of business names, and then complete the registration procedure at the clerk's window.

Business Name Brainstorming

List three ideas based on the type of service you plan to provide (e.g., dental, quality, assured):

1. _____

2. _____

3. _____

List three ideas based on your geographic location (e.g., the name of your town, county, or state):

1. _____

2. _____

3. _____

List three ideas based on a local feature (e.g., mountain; seaside; historical reference, like Alamo; or even botanical feature, if that's what your area is known for or you like, such as Magnolia or Rose or Chaparral):

1. _____

2. _____

3. _____

Now, after you've decided which name you like the best, have you:

❑ Tried it aloud to make sure it's easily understood and pronounced? (Has it passed muster with your family? Have you had a friend call to see how it sounds over the phone?)

❑ Checked your local Yellow Pages to make sure the same or similar name is not already listed?

❑ Checked with your local business name authority to make sure it's available?

❑ Checked the internet to see if someone else is using it as a domain? (See sidebar, "Of Surf and Scoping a Name," on page 90.)

Good! Now register it and make it your own.

FIGURE 5–1: **Business Name Brainstorming**

Your Skeletal Structure

To appease those picky IRS people, your business must have a structure. You can operate it as a sole proprietorship, a partnership, or a corporation, with variations thereon. Most medical billing services go with the simplest version, the sole proprietorship. You'll probably be starting out on your own, so there's no need to get complicated or expensive. You can always switch to another format later on if and when you take on partners and/or employees.

The Walnut Creek MIB restructured her business as a partnership. She had been self-employed in the field for about nine years when her accountants—who helped set up her sole proprietorship at the beginning of her MIB career—asked to become her partners. (See the checklist in Figure 5–2 for help with covering the basics when structuring your own business.)

warning

Just liking somebody is not a good enough reason to go into a partnership. "You've got to see what each brings to the table," Mary V. cautions. Make sure that you and your potential partner have strengths that complement each other.

Structuring Your Business

Use this handy checklist to make sure you've covered all the governmental regulatory bases.

Yes! I have:

- ❏ Filed a fictitious business name

- ❏ Decided on whether to become a sole proprietorship, partnership, or corporation

- ❏ Filed the necessary forms to become a partnership or corporation, if that's what I chose

- ❏ Applied for a local business license

- ❏ Checked into zoning regulations

- ❏ Complied with the following special rules, if any, that need my attention:

  _____

  _____

  _____

- ❏ Checked into local privacy laws

FIGURE 5–2: **Structuring Your Business**

► Domain, Please

Whether or not you plan on developing a website for your business (see Chapter 10), check the internet to see if someone else is already using your company's name as a domain. If so, consider coming up with something else so that your clients will not be confused if they try to find you online. Then hurry up and register it before someone else snags it!

New domain registrations can cost as little as $10 annually. This also generally includes free parking (in the absence of a website), a free business email account, and other ecommerce options. Try www.GoDaddy.com or www.Register.com to see what names are available.

Ideally, your domain name should be the same as your medical claims billing service. However, if the name is too long or already taken, think of something else that still accurately reflects the nature of your business. This will also give you the opportunity to crank up those creative juices and have some fun when thinking of business names. (Incidentally, the name "Creative Juices" has been used for several businesses.)

Mary V., who started her business as a partnership, changed gears and established a limited liability corporation (LLC) when the relationship with her business partner went sour. ("I was doing all the work," she says.) But at the beginning, the partnership worked well because the two women didn't step on each other's toes. Mary handled the customer service and technical side of the business while her partner, who had a background in insurance sales, took charge of selling. "I didn't like her side," Mary confesses, "and she hated my side." That made the blending of their skills a perfect combination.

Home Zoned Home

If you plan on a home office, you should check into zoning regulations, even though medical billing is not a business that's going to attract a lot of attention from the authorities. You won't need signage, and you'll rarely have clients knocking on your door, so you don't need to worry about parking restrictions. But it's still a good idea to play it safe. Find out from your local government whether any permits are necessary.

"I don't have people coming and going," the Montana MIB says. "I don't offer a product; I offer a service." Therefore, she met the local municipality's guidelines for residential businesses. All she was required to obtain was the usual business license.

Speaking of which, while you're querying the local authorities, you should ask about a business license. There is generally a nominal annual fee for this, but it's easier to get the license than to ignore it and worry about it in the back of your mind.

Strange Fees

The quintessential MIB rarely has to be concerned with any fees or licenses other than the ones we've just discussed. Every once in a strange while, however, something weird this way comes.

When the Walnut Creek, California, MIB started her business, "There was what we'll call a governing agency for collection agencies and billing services for the state of California," she recalls, "and their dues were $1,000 a year. To be looked upon kindly by the physicians' community, you really had to be covered by that agency, so I paid my dues. And about three months later they went out of business." Fortunately, she has a sense of humor. Also fortunately, this sort of story is extremely rare.

> **tip** ⓘ
>
> Always get a name, department, and phone extension when you speak to someone in officialdom. This can save you hours of re-explanation later if you need to call back. Plus, you make a buddy who can help later down the line.

Loose Lips Sink Ships

While we're discussing legalese, let's go over the issue of patient confidentiality. Your doctors will trust you not only with their income but in some cases with their patients' most intimate secrets. You must uphold "your" patients' legal rights to privacy at all times, regardless of how titillating—or humdrum—you think their stories are.

As a medical biller/coder, you will most likely have access to patients' electronic health records (EHR), which is a digital version of a patient's paper chart. The coolest thing about an EHR is that health information can be shared with other providers and organizations such as labs, pharmacies, and hospitals. These records typically include the patient's medical history with diagnoses, medications, images, and test results. This makes it easier for everyone to be on the same page when treating a patient. It also means you will be privy to a lot of sensitive information.

The bottom line is, don't give in to the temptation to gab about anybody's personal, medical, or financial life to anybody except the doctor and his staff. And even then it should only be in the most professional terms.

Become familiar with the federal and state privacy laws in your area. Your local hospital's medical records department, which must comply with stringent guidelines, or your local medical society should be able to give you information pertinent to your area.

HIPAA, HIPAA. . . Oh No!

There's an even more compelling reason these days to keep those medical records private and confidential. Just when you thought it wasn't possible for our government to dream up any more new regulations, along comes HIPAA, or the Health Insurance Portability and Accountability Act of 1996. This 500-page privacy rule was devised by the Department of Health and Human Services during the Clinton administration. It provides federal protection for personal health information so it can't be used for nonhealth purposes (like denying employment), as well as a host of other reasons.

Every vendor who comes into contact with protected health information, from MIBs to IT vendors, copy services, recyclers, shredders, and others, have to adhere to the same high standards regarding confidentiality under the provisions of HIPAA. While the onus for protecting health information actually falls on the physician offices, hospitals, or other medical sources (known collectively as "covered entities") that provide you with the data you need for medical billing, MIBs must remember that everything has to be encrypted and kept confidential, including any electronic health records you work with.

Under HIPAA's provisions, covered entities are required to have any vendors (like you) who handle their protected records sign a "business associate contract" before sensitive health information is passed along. According to Mary Ray Brophy, Esq., an employee health benefits attorney in the Greater Detroit area, such contracts permit the covered entity to disclose protected health information to a business associate as long as the associate agrees that the information will only be used as specified in the agreement or by law. These are some of the terms and conditions you may want to consider including:

▶ A description of the exact way the business associate is permitted to use and/or disclose protected health information. For an MIB business associate contract, this might be as simple as stating, "Use is restricted to coding medical conditions for the express purpose of generating a bill for each patient's insurance company."

▶ An agreement not to use or disclose protected health information for any reason other than the reasons listed in the business associate contract. That gives the covered entity the right to terminate the contract if, say, you leak details about a famous basketball player's embarrassing health problem to a supermarket tabloid newspaper.

▶ A discussion of the safeguards the vendor will take when working with protected health information. For an MIB, that might mean outlining whether you have a formal security and privacy program (fairly simple for a one-person home-based business), whether you will use record encryption, how you will receive and transmit electronic data, and so on.

warning

Obviously, medical billers will have to comply with HIPAA, but it won't be an onerous task.

▶ A guarantee that the business associate's own vendors (like your 17-year-old part-time file clerk or your document-shredding company) will abide by the same conditions and restrictions that the Business Associate must follow (a huge issue as it relates to your file clerk and the aforementioned basketball player).

▶ A host of other stuff the covered entity's legal team might deem necessary.

You can find out more information about provisions that might be included in a business associate contract on the U.S. Department of Health and Human Services site at: www.hhs.gov/ocr/hipaa/contractprov.html. If you find yourself dateless on a Friday night, you also can try typing "business associate contract" in your web browser to see what pops up. A recent attempt on the Google browser yielded more than 6,530,000 hits, so obviously there's plenty of information out there already. The same goes for searching on "HIPAA." Just about everyone who has anything to do with health care currently has a HIPAA link on his or her website.

So what does all this really mean for MIBs? "Obviously, medical billers will have to comply with HIPAA, but it won't be an onerous task," says Brophy, who presents seminars on HIPAA and privacy rules and their effect on employers. "While the business associate contract will include a lot of requirements that billers will have to follow, if the agreements are properly drafted and enforced, most will find that all they have to do is follow good business practices." Most physician offices will have a standard contract you can sign, but it is always advisable to provide one of your own, just to cover your bases.

Some of those commonsense work practices include turning off your computer, securing access to protected documents, and otherwise safeguarding patient information on your screen when you walk away from your desk.

And just in case you're wondering, the penalties for violating HIPAA can be stiff. Fines start at $100 per violation for the inadvertent disclosure of information (like mistakenly allowing your nosy neighbor to glimpse sensitive records on your computer screen that would be of interest to the local media). On the high side, violators could face a $250,000 fine and ten years in the slammer for willful and wanton disclosure of protected information, such as selling protected information to a person who's fact-finding for a client involved in a malpractice suit.

The bottom line is, "Don't slip up—do the HIPAA!"

Your Business Gurus

It never hurts to consult an attorney and accountant for tips on how to proceed with your business structure. Your attorney and accountant will be able to help you determine what is best for your particular situation.

You'll also want an attorney to look over the contracts you'll be signing with doctors and to advise you on any special concerns (read "worries and anxieties")—like malpractice, a doctor or government entity accusing you of fraudulent coding or billing, or a patient who sues for no good reason.

Don't forget your insurance agent. She can ease the same worries and concerns by providing errors and omissions coverage as well as special protection for your business equipment.

The MIBs from Minnesota and Napa also recommend finding a mentor to help walk you through the process of starting a medical claims billing service. Sandra S. says that she has a phenomenal mentor. "She was my supervisor when I worked for an insurance company, and is the smartest woman I know." Heidi H. had a much harder time finding someone who would talk to her about the business industry. "They saw me as a threat," she says. "Finally, I was able to talk to a lady who started out of her home. She was kind enough to answer some of my questions and eventually became a mentor. She really helped me out with ideas and pointing me in the right direction. Because of that I like to pay it forward and also help people starting out in the industry."

We've given you an x-ray of the typical medical billing service's skeleton. The licenses, fees, and structures discussed are the only ones you should need to worry about.

Figuring Your Finances

That old refrain "The best things in life are free" does not quite apply when you're starting a business. This chapter, therefore, dips into the murky waters of budgeting, financing, and operating costs and, like chlorine, clears them up.

Startup Costs

One of the many nifty things about a medical billing service is that its startup costs are comparatively low. You have the advantage of establishing a homebased business, which cuts office lease expenses down to nothing. You have almost no inventory, which means no outlay of funds for pretty doodads to grace display spaces. (And in fact, you have no display spaces!) Your major financial outlay will be for office equipment and your software and/or business opportunity since, if you're like many moderns, you already have a computer.

But let's take it from the top. The following is a breakdown of everything—from heavy investment pieces to flyweight items—you'll need to get up and running:

- ▶ Computer system with an internet connection and printer
- ▶ Fax machine
- ▶ Software and/or business opportunity
- ▶ Clearinghouse
- ▶ Reference materials
- ▶ CMS 1500 forms
- ▶ Phone
- ▶ Voice mail or answering machine
- ▶ Stationery and office supplies
- ▶ Postage

You can add all kinds of goodies of varying degrees of necessity onto this list, and we'll cover all of them in depth in Chapter 9—a sort of shopping bonanza. For example, a copier is a plus. It's also nice to have bona fide office furniture: a tweedy upholstered chair with lumbar support that swivels and rolls, gleaming file cabinets that really lock, real oak bookshelves.

But let's consider that you're starting absolutely from scratch. You can always set up your computer on your kitchen table or on a card table in a corner of the bedroom. You can stash files in cardboard boxes. It's not glamorous, but it'll suffice until you get your business steaming ahead. You can garner patient materials by post instead of by fax, as some MIBs have opted to do.

Computing Computer Costs

A computer is absolutely essential for any type of business. Not only do you need it to process claims, it can also help you manage bookkeeping and inventory control tasks, maintain client records, and produce marketing materials. At a minimum, you'll need a premium desktop computer, the most current version of Windows, and 2 GB to 16 GB RAM (with 8 GB being the sweet spot). Depending on your needs, you can expect to pay from $1,000 to $2,500 for a good brand-name computer, including a monitor, mouse, and printer.

We'll go over all the permutations in the next chapter, but this will give you a figure to pencil in for starters.

save

Just about any type of secondhand business equipment can be purchased for a fraction of its original retail cost. Shop the online auctions, check the classified ad section of your local newspaper, and ask new equipment dealers if they have trade-ins or repossessions for sale. Careful shopping for preowned items can save hundreds of dollars.

The Cyberspace Connection

High-speed internet service basically goes along with the computer because it is essential to have access to the internet. Invest in the fastest high-speed internet service that your budget will allow if you anticipate transmitting a high volume of information on a regular basis. The cost for internet service widely varies with monthly costs starting at $20.

Fax Facts

Although technically you don't have to have a fax machine, your MIB life will run much more smoothly with one. You can shoot off and receive materials to and from doctors, carriers, and patients instead of waiting on the postal service. Sending a claim follow-up by fax, for example, has a lot more impact on the insurer when it directly follows your call. You can purchase a basic plain-paper fax machine for as little as $100.

The Skinny on Software

Software prices can vary radically, depending on which medical claims billing package you buy and from whom. This is an area to which you should devote a great deal of research. You're going to be virtually married to your program, spending hours of quality time with it, and you want to be sure you and your software are a match made in microprocessing heaven. Again, this is a subject we'll discuss in depth in Chapter 9.

Let's say here that you'll want to allocate somewhere between $500 and $5,000, depending on many variables, including whether you purchase just the MIB software or the business opportunity to go with it.

The MIB in New Jersey started with low-end software. While she was still in typewriter mode, she happened upon a catalog and began flipping through it. "I went to the Medical

Arts Press catalog and I picked software for $499—didn't even know the name of it—and had it shipped," she laughs. "I don't know if I was brave or ignorant. I didn't actually know there were other people doing medical insurance billing."

After she'd been up and running a while with the "blind date" software and became more industry-savvy, she switched to a full business opportunity/software package.

Clearinghouse Costs

Clearinghouses, like software, require research on your part. If the software is like a marriage partner or significant other, then the clearinghouse is the brother- or sister-in-law that comes to visit for what seems to be the rest of your life. You'd better be sure you're happy living under the same roof with it.

Many times you can find the software and clearinghouse integrated in the same package, which ensures their compatibility. Otherwise, you will want to make sure the clearinghouse is going to live in harmony with your billing software or you will live in what is known as "clearinghouse hell." This happens when there is a claim error and the clearinghouse blames the software company, who blames the clearinghouse, and back and forth until someone takes responsibility. Try to avoid that at all costs.

Also like software, clearinghouse costs vary radically. You should allocate from zero to $300 for "membership" fees and from zero to $100 per doctor for sign-up.

By Way of Reference

Although your reference library can comfortably contain a wealth of texts, we'll consider here only the very few that are real must-haves: the ICD-10, CPT, and HCPCS Level II Expert coding books. If you're billing for dentists, you'll also want the CDT codes, which is the dental version of CPT codes. You can sketch in about $100 for a single download of CPT or around $250 if you have a small staff of under ten people and wish to network the software. The CPT and CDT physical books cost around $105 and $75, respectively. While the ICD-10 Second Edition classification codes can be accessed for free (see the Appendix), figure on spending around $150 for the HCPCS Level II Expert.

The Napa MIB prefers hardcopy books in lieu of downloads, which are sometimes a little pricier. She has also added an NDC directory (National Drug Code), which has every injectable that a doctor might use. "This can be especially useful if you are working for a family practice or dermatologist," she says. The MIB from Minnesota also recommends having a medical terminology dictionary on hand. A couple of online sources are listed in the Appendix.

Phone Fun

We assume that you already have a telephone, in which case you already know all about phone bills. You should, however, install at least one separate dedicated landline for your business, maybe two. You'll want one line for handling phone calls and another for your fax transmissions, unless you plan to transmit all your information late at night or in the wee hours of morning. Fax machines use phones the way teenagers do—when they're transmitting, no one else can possibly get through. So unless you want to risk having callers receive a busy signal or empty ring when you're faxing claims, you'll want to have a separate line.

Costs, of course, depend on how many fun features you add to your telephone service and which local and long-distance carriers you go with, but for the purpose of startup budgeting, let's say you should allocate about $25 per line. You'll also need to add the phone company's installation fee, which should be around $50. Check with your local Ma Bell (or one of her deregulated relatives) to determine exactly what these costs are in your area.

Another alternative is to use a cloud communications system like RingCentral that can handle all or some of your communication needs such as a "soft phone," answering machine, fax, and texts on multiple devices. Although the Napa MIB uses RingCentral as her company's answering machine and to send/receive secure faxes, she recommends a landline phone. "I prefer the handheld because I like to slam the receiver," she laughs. "It's good stress relief!"

Please Leave a Message

You will occasionally want to escape from your telephone—when you're out seeing clients, running errands, or (when you have everything caught up) skipping off to the movies. During these times, you will need somebody or something to answer your phone. A Murphy's Law of Business Life is that people call most often when: a) you are not in your office, b) you are sitting down to a meal, or c) you are in the shower.

Another business life law is that an unanswered phone is extremely unprofessional. "Having an answering machine or voice mail is important," says the Napa MIB. "Doctors don't like to make a lot of calls, so they need to know what their options are if they can't reach you right away such as leaving a detailed message and knowing you will respond."

You have several ways to go here: the trusty answering machine, the phone company's voice mail feature, or a cloud-based communication system mentioned earlier. All have pros and cons, which we'll discuss in Chapter 9. For estimating startup costs, let's figure a basic answering machine at about $40, voice mail at about $6 a month, or the cloud-based answering service starting around $25 a month.

Office Supplies

Business stationery is as important to a crisp, efficient image as a professionally answered phone. To create that efficient identity—which will be one of your biggest selling points—you'll need letterhead, envelopes, and business cards. There are a lot of routes to take with all this stuff.

Let's say, however, that to create the basics, you can purchase blank stationery, including cards, and print them up yourself with your word-processing or desktop publishing program. Or you can have a set of business cards inexpensively printed for you at a quick-print house like FedEx Office or at Office Depot's in-house service. Online printing services such as Vistaprint can also provide snazzy designs for a nominal fee.

"I spent $49 for a thousand business cards," the Virginia MIB says. "I maybe have used, I would say, not over 20 of them. The rest of it's been word-of-mouth."

Office supplies—pens, pencils, paper clips, colored pickup folders or mailing envelopes for your clients, reams of blank paper for designing brochures or fliers, stapler, staples, letter opener, tape, printer cartridges—can be penciled in at about $150. This is, of course, if you start from absolute scratch, buying everything brand-new for your business. CMS 1500 forms go for less than $35 for a box of 2,500.

Postage

We're not talking the Victoria's Secret catalog mailroom here. Your postage costs will be fairly low, but you do need to tally them into your startup costs. How much you spend depends a great deal on what you expect to be doing. If you supply each doctor with a priority mail envelope each week, as the San Diego MIB does, then your costs to receive material will run approximately $22-$25 a month per doctor. If you figure paper claims and patient statements at 300 pieces per doctor per month, then you'll spend another $135 or more per month to mail out statements.

tip

If your budget can stretch that far, it's a good idea to talk to an accountant and an attorney. They can advise you on tax issues before tax time, make sure your client contract is up to snuff, and generally keep you out of trouble.

save

"[Postage] is a reimbursable expense," the Denver MIB says firmly. "Our physicians pay their own postage." She charges mail costs back to each doctor, but she also gives them a break by batching claims to various carriers together, thus saving money.

You should also calculate how much it will cost to send out brochures or other direct-mail pieces. If you send out five a week, you will spend roughly another $15 a month.

Postage Meters and Internet Postage

Once your business is up and running and you find yourself handling a lot of outgoing mail such as bills sent to clients and brochures sent to new prospects, consider leasing a postage meter, which can be a huge time-saver. Not only does it eliminate those annoying and nonproductive trips to and from the post office (not to mention the long waits in line), but it also saves you from licking and sticking stamps on envelopes.

Postage meters allow you to pay for postage in advance and print the exact amount on the mailing piece when it is used. Meters also provide a "big company" professional image, are more convenient than stamps, and can save you money in a number of ways. Postage meters are leased, not sold, with rates starting at about $20 per month. They require a license, which is available from your local post office. Only four manufacturers are licensed by the U.S. Postal Service to manufacture and lease postage meters; your local post office can provide you with contact information. You may find that buying postage online (check out www.Stamps.com) is an affordable and convenient alternative to a postage meter. You also may need a postal scale to make sure you're affixing enough postage to your outgoing mail. A first-class stamp covers letters of up to 1 ounce, which is roughly three to four pages of letter-sized paper. Anything over that requires additional postage. Some of the online companies will provide you with a postal scale free or for a nominal charge. Otherwise, you can expect to pay $20 to $60 for a mechanical scale (which is useful if you mail up to 12 items a day) or $50 to $200 for a digital scale for sending 12 to 24 items per day. If you send more than 24 items a day or use priority or expedited mailing services on a regular basis, you should consider purchasing a programmable electronic scale, which runs $80 to $300.

Adding It All Up

Use the worksheet in Figure 6–2 on page 113 to pencil in and then tally up all your costs. If you copy a couple of extra sheets first, you can compare various options, decide which will work the best for you, and then arrive at your "Official Startup Figure."

The New Jersey MIB estimated her original startup costs at close to $5,000 or $6,000. She did not include her final choice software package in this figure because she purchased it after she'd already been up and running.

The Montana MIB put her startup costs in the same range. With this amount, she was able to purchase her training, software, computer, and the necessary office furniture.

The former pastor's costs were higher. Figuring in purchasing a fax machine, upgrading his existing home office, and spending about $700 to print brochures, he weighed in his total startup at just a little more than $10,000.

Talking Money

Now that we've determined how much it's going to cost you to get your business up and running, let's turn to the fun part—figuring out how much money you can expect to make.

Medical billing services charge their clients by three methods: percentage, per claim, and hourly. The percentage basis is generally used by MIBs who do full-practice management or a combination of patient billing and claims billing and, just as it sounds, the MIB charges the provider a percentage of the money he *collects* per month as opposed to the amount of money he *bills*.

"We charge [the doctors] on collected revenues, not on their production levels," the Walnut Creek, California, MIB explains. "The money all comes to us and we put it into their own personal checking accounts and then I will bill them, depending on how big the practice is, sometimes twice a month, sometimes once a month. And they pay the bill in a timely manner or we stop doing their work."

The percentages you'll charge will depend on several variables: the going rate in your part of the country, the sorts of procedures your doctors are providing, and their patient volume.

"I take a lot of things into consideration," Maryland-based Mary V. says. "With what I know about certain things, I'll charge the doctor a different percentage on the type of claim that it is. I charge a different percentage for workers' comp, for personal injury. If they handle a lot of cash, I'll actually drop that percentage because I know I'm not going to have to bill that out. All I'm going to do is data entry. One doctor might have four different percentages. With experience, I know now how much time certain claims take. With personal injury, it might be six years before that case is settled."

Since personal injury cases take so long to pay, Mary charges a higher percentage of the claim, usually 10 percent and above, whereas routine Medicare claims are billed at anywhere from 5 percent to 10 percent.

With all these variables, estimating an annual income might seem like a task fit for a professor of Boolean mathematics, but it's not really difficult. In fact, it's fun! (Adding up numbers is always more interesting when it pertains to money in your bank account.)

Here's what you do: First, settle on an average percentage. Let's use 7 percent, which is the fee the San Diego MIB charges.

stat fact

Paper claims cost $3 to $18 each to process, while electronic transmissions cost just pennies, according to *Health Data Management* magazine.

Next, estimate how much one client will collect in a year. This is tough, starting cold, because you don't have any clients to base your figures on. If you've done your homework, however, you'll have an idea of how much money doctors in your target market are billing and collecting per month.

Let's say your first doctor collects a nice round figure of $21,000 per month, which multiplied by 12 months gives him an annual collectable income of $252,000. His billable income might be far more, and this, of course, is where you come in—your mission being to bring his billable and collectable into alignment.

Now, all you have to do is multiply this $252,000 current collectable figure by 7 percent, which gives you a potential annual income of $17,640. We say "potential" because this sum, as we've just explained, can improve dramatically once you're at the helm. For example, if you're able to increase the doctor's collectable income by 10 percent, he'll now be bringing in $277,000 per year, which will give you $19,404 per year.

If you increase your client base by another five providers, each with the same collectable income, you're suddenly grossing $116,424 per year.

Per-Claim Jumping

Some MIBs prefer to charge on a per-claim basis rather than by percentage (anywhere from $3 to $10 per claim). This is the method of choice for billers whose workload consists mainly of straight claims billing with little or no practice management tasks.

"I bill per claim," says the Illinois MIB. "The offices do the front-end data entry and I do the back-end tweaking and electronic filing and some of the follow-up work. I'm charging right now anywhere from $5 to $8 per claim."

In rural Virginia, the teacher charges $4.50 per insurance claim and $3.75 per patient invoice, which she feels is probably average in her area. Up in suburban New Jersey, another MIB charges $7 to $10 per claim.

When you charge via this method, you charge per claim billed rather than per claim collected. You will want to charge the going rate in your area, which you'll have determined through the market research we discussed

fun fact ☺

When speaking finances, gross does not indicate something, like, totally disgusting, dude. It refers to the amount you earn before you deduct expenses. Net is the amount of income after expenses are deducted.

▶ Reserves, Not Just for Feds

Some medical billing services take off immediately, usually because they have built-in business, that is someone who's already requested their services. Others struggle for months before landing that first client. If you have providers already lined up, you can skip this section. But if you're starting cold with the only active clients the ones in your mind's eye, then you'll need to determine what sort of financial reserves will be necessary to keep you eating until your business gets going.

It took the San Diego MIB five months to land her first client. This is not unusual in this business. In fact, it's a given that nabbing those first doctors is a tough proposition. Unless you have a trust fund or a significant other bringing home the bacon, don't quit your day job.

With a brand-new client in the stable, the former nurse is figuring an average monthly gross of about $700 and operating expenses of under $150. Kim H., who's still working as a teacher, earns $800 to $1,000 a month with minimal monthly expenses and is not yet prepared to give up her day job.

in Chapter 4. Since you'll also have determined through your research how many claims doctors in your area are filing each month, you'll have a good basis for determining your annual gross income.

Let's say your first doctor is billing 350 claims per month, which, multiplied by 12 months, comes to 4,200 claims. If you charge $5 per claim, your gross annual income will be $21,000. Now, if you take on another five physicians, your gross jumps to $126,000.

Counting the Hours

The third, and least popular, method of charging clients is per hour. The San Diego biller feels this may be a hard selling feature for most doctors. "They're already paying somebody on an hourly basis. Why would they want to hire somebody outside the office and pay them hourly as well?"

You might want to consider this option if you have a client whose billing rate is so low that charging per claim or on a percentage basis is not feasible. Or you might run into a client who is comfortable working under this arrangement and does not want to deviate from her norm.

tip

If you are figuring an hourly charge, make sure the fee you set is comparable to per-claim or percentage rates—enough to make the work worth your effort.

Your market research will be one of the keys to determining an hourly charge. Here is one way to determine an hourly rate. Let's take an average of your annual fee for one doctor, based on the per-claim and percentage methods we used above. This will give us an annual gross income of $20,000. Now, if we divide this by 12 months, we get $1,667 per month. Assuming that your client supplies only 40 hours of work a month, you end up with an hourly charge of $42.

(Note that these are all hypothetical figures. You may far exceed these numbers, or you may find that your economic region, your level of expertise, or the amount of work you choose to do puts your income somewhere below what we've given.)

Operating Expenses

OK, we've had a ball counting chickens. Now it's time to swing the pendulum the other way and calculate your operating expenses. These, subtracted from your projected gross income, will tell the true tale of how much you'll be making.

We will assume once again that you are going to be homebased, so we won't worry about expenses for office rent or utilities. However, we do need to think about the following:

▶ Phone

▶ Postage

▶ Stationery and office supplies

▶ Clearinghouse

▶ Loan repayment

▶ Online service

The MIBs interviewed for this book feel that their operating expenses are minimal. "I would say that I can run everything for less than $250 a month," the MIB in Montana says, "and that would include postage, paper, telephone, and internet service. I have very few expenses."

The Illinois MIB says, "Now that I've got pretty much everything I needed, [my operating expenses] are low. It really just depends on how many claims I process because obviously the clearinghouses charge you per claim. So if you take that out of the picture, it's pretty much just a bigger phone bill." He estimates his monthly phone charges, with two lines, at about $89 a month.

> **tip** (i)
>
> Now that you have done the math, you can also figure your gross profit margin—your operating expenses divided by your earnings. As with profits themselves in the MIB industry, gross profit margins have a wide range, depending largely on whether commercial office space expenses and employee expenses are involved.

▶ Mix 'n' Match

The great fun of all these charge methods is that you can mix and match methods and rates, customizing each doctor's contract. "Most everything I do is per claim," the New Jersey MIB says. "But I do have two psychiatrists on a percentage basis, between 7 [percent] and 9 percent. I base every practice differently."

You can beef up your monthly charges—and cover some of your startup expenses—by customizing other featured services for your providers. You can charge your doctors a one-time setup fee for entering their patients into your software program. You could accomplish this by charging a flat fee, say $300, the same setup fee you may be charged by your clearinghouse. This will neatly cancel out one startup expense from your list. Or you might charge your doctors per existing patient, say $4 each. If each doctor in your stable of six has an average of 400 patients, then you've added $9,600 of extra income.

The first three items on the list—phone, postage, and stationery/supplies—have been covered in this chapter's startup section. Your monthly operating expenses should be about the same as we've discussed.

Cuckoo for Clearinghouses

Your clearinghouse expenses will be different. Once you pay your origination fee and your per-doctor fee, you'll be looking at the per-claim fee. If, for example, the clearinghouse you choose charges 50 cents per claim and you plan to route through 150 claims per month, then you'll need to pencil in $75.

All of this is subject, of course, to any number of variations. For instance, the Montana MIB's clearinghouse charges a flat fee of $40 for an unlimited number of claims. The Maryland MIB's clearinghouse charges 35 cents per claim. And the clearinghouse used in conjunction with one business opportunity vendor has no fees unless you process fewer than 400 claims per month. The Georgia MIB says to make sure the clearinghouse you are looking at offers "drop to paper claims," and find out how much they charge for paper claims. Her favorite clearinghouse is Zirmed (http://public.zirmed.com). "Of all the ones I've worked with in the past two years, they have the easiest claims correction and resubmission functionality," says Marsha S.

Keep in mind that not all your claims will be sent electronically, and of those that are, not all will go through a clearinghouse. You can bill directly to Medicare and the Blues.

Startup Scenarios

In Figure 6–1, page 112, check out the startup costs (in other words, the costs to officially throw open door) for two hypothetical billing services: Check-Up Medical Billing and Health-Care Help Services. Check-Up is a homebased company (office in the spare bedroom) whose owner is retired and decided to start out small with a minimum outlay. Health-Care, on the other hand, has rented a 500-square-foot downtown office, purchased top-of-the-line equipment, and employed a part-time assistant. Check-Up is projecting annual gross collections of $16,800; Health-Care's annual projection is $42,000. Neither owner draws a salary; instead, they take a percentage of their net profits as income. Figure 6–2 on page 113 is a worksheet for your use.

Paying the Piper

We've set aside an operating expense called loan repayment. If you don't borrow money to start your business, you won't need this one. If, however, you finance your startup costs through any means, you'll need to repay the piper, and here's where you pencil in whatever your monthly fee is.

Olé for Online Service

This expense is a must-have if you want to take advantage of the ease and affordability of online claim processing. Again, your costs will depend on which service you go with and what rate you choose, but the majority have given up on competing rate-wise and routinely charge $20 to $60 a month for unlimited usage.

Putting It All Together

You can use the worksheet in Figure 6–4 on page 117 to pencil in your projected income and estimated operating expenses. You may have many more expenses than the ones discussed here, such as yearly coding upgrades, seminars and their requisite travel expenses, employees and their requisite workers' compensation insurance, pension plans, auto expenses, subscription fees for professional journals, butler and maid service (just dreaming!), and pizza delivery or Chinese take-out costs.

> **tip** ⓘ
>
> No one can tell you how many claims any client will generate; there are too many variables. But Tammy Harlan, president/ CEO of Medical Billing Course, LLC, a medical billing training company, says the average family practice doctor has approximately 500 claims per month.

Startup Expenses

Expenses	Check-Up Medical Billing	Health-Care Help Services
Rent (security deposit and first month)	$N/A	$1,000.00
Office equipment, furniture, & supplies	3,083.00	8,905.00
Postage meter (rent for one year)	N/A	180.00
MIB software	700.00	N/A
MIB software/business opportunity package	N/A	5,000.00
Clearinghouse startup fees	300.00	N/A
CMS 1500 forms	35.00	35.00
Licenses	150.00	150.00
Phone/internet	90.00	115.00
Utility deposits	N/A	150.00
Employee wages	N/A	875.00
Grand opening advertising	100.00	500.00
Legal services	375.00	525.00
Insurance	500.00	600.00
Subtotal	**$5,368.00**	**$17,990.00**
Miscellaneous expenses (add roughly 10% of total)	$537.00	$1,799.00
Total Startup Costs	**$5,870.00**	**$19,834.00**

FIGURE 6–1: **Startup Expenses for Two Hypothetical Businesses**

Startup Expenses Worksheet

Expenses	Cost
Rent (security deposit and first month)	$
Office equipment and furniture *(see MIB Office Checklist, Figure 9–1 on page 137)*	
Postage meter (rent for one year)	
MIB software	
MIB software/business opportunity	
Clearinghouse startup fees	
Reference materials	
CMS 1500 forms	
Licenses	
Phone/internet	
Utility deposits	
Employees	
Grand opening advertising	
Legal and accounting services	
Insurance	
Subtotal	
Miscellaneous expenses	
Official Startup Figure	$

FIGURE 6–2: **Startup Expenses Worksheet**

We've put in rent, utilities, employee, and insurance costs, but obviously, if these don't apply to you, don't worry about them.

Once you've calculated your estimated operating expenses you can subtract them from your calculated earnings and–voilà!–you have a projected income/expense total.

Help from Your Friends

Now that you've done all the arithmetic, you can determine just how much you'll need to get started. Why, then, you may ask, did I have to go through all the work of figuring out my net income?

Good question. The answer is that, first off, you'll now have determined that it's worth borrowing money to get started in this business. And second, you can show all these beautifully executed figures to your borrower to show him or her that your business is a good risk and that you'll be able to repay the loan without difficulty.

Another of the many joys of the medical billing service is that its startup costs are relatively low. Some MIBs were able to finance themselves with assistance only from a friendly little plastic rectangle.

"I had a partner when I first got into the business, and we financed it using credit cards," Mary V. says. "Nobody would give us a loan, so it was credit cards. My partner and I were sitting one night [working] and somebody called us from my alma mater and said, 'We want you to have a credit card,' and I thought 'Wow, OK!' That's how we started. That's how we bought a lot of things."

The Montana MIB went the same route. "I went ahead and put [the startup financing] on a card with a very low interest rate, and it was less than I could have received a business loan for," she says.

"I was in a slightly different situation from most people," the Walnut Creek MIB recalls of her startup financing experiences years ago. "I had just completed a divorce, we had done our financial settlement, and we had sold a house, so I took the money from the house and put it in the business." But it still wasn't enough.

"I couldn't find funding," the former nurse says. "I was a female with no business experience. So I just went on a wing and a prayer."

When her accountants—the ones who have since become her partners—first heard her plans, their reaction was "Oh my God, you'll never make it. It's not possible, you're underfunded."

"And I really was underfunded," the Walnut Creek MIB adds. "It was a huge struggle, but I had two employees who knew me, who knew how well I could do, and put their total faith in me, left good secure jobs to come with me. And I didn't take a salary for almost a year. It was kind of interesting. It was a true struggle, but I managed to land a very, very good client, an orthopedic group with five doctors on board who understood what I was trying to do and who hung in there with me."

The Illinois MIB financed his startup by going to a familiar source: his father. He didn't have to do a big sales pitch, he says. "I let him know what I was doing and why I wanted to do it."

Most MIBs, like the ex-pastor, are self-financed, via Visa or MasterCard, relatives, or on-hand cash.

> **tip** ⓘ
>
> Take advantage of the abundance of local, state, and federal programs designed to support small businesses. Make your first stop the Small Business Administration; then investigate various other programs.

Romancing the Bank

You might want to consider financing through your bank or credit union. In this case, your startup cost and income figures are extremely important. The bank will want to see all of this, neatly laid out and carefully calculated. You'll also want to show them your mission statement, business plan, and any figures you can present—for instance, the ones in this book—about the bright future of the medical billing industry.

If you do go with a bank, it may pay to think small. "Small banks traditionally are better for small businesses because they're always looking for ways to accommodate these customers," said Wendy Thomas, senior business consultant at the Michigan Small Business Development Center in Detroit. "Small banks may be more willing to deal with small-business concerns and are more sensitive to issues like the need for longer accounts receivable periods."

Income and Expense Operations

In Figure 6–3, page 116, take a look at the sample Operating Income/Expenses. We've provided a worksheet in Figure 6–4, page 117. Use it to compute your projected income and expenses.

Instead of shooting for a straight business loan, the prospective MIB could go for a home equity loan or borrow against a vehicle that's paid for or a savings or CD account. Don't discount your home as a cash cow—you might be surprised to learn how much equity you actually have.

Get the lowdown on getting financing for your business—from friends and family to credit cards and bank loans.

Operating Income/Expenses

Projected Monthly Income			$5,000.00
Projected Monthly Expenses			
	Phone/internet	$40.00	
	Postage	50.00	
	Miscellaneous expenses *(stationery and office supplies)*	50.00	
	Rent	625.00	
	Utilities	50.00	
	Employees	540.00	
	Advertising	200.00	
	Clearinghouse fees	120.00	
	Insurance	75.00	
	Loan repayment	250.00	
	Online service	50.00	
Total Expenses			−$2,050.00
Projected Income/Expense Total			**$2,950.00**

Note: *Sound accounting practice dictates that you allow six months' operating expenses as your suggested operating capital.*

FIGURE 6–3: **Operating Income/Expenses**

Operating Income/Expenses Worksheet

Projected Monthly Income			$	
Projected Monthly Expenses				
	Phone/internet	$		
	Postage			
	Miscellaneous expenses *(stationery and office supplies)*			
	Rent			
	Utilities			
	Employees			
	Advertising			
	Clearinghouse fees			
	Insurance			
	Loan repayment			
	Online service			
Total Expenses			$–	
Projected Income/Expense Total			$	

Note: *Sound accounting practice dictates that you allow six months' operating expenses as your suggested operating capital.*

FIGURE 6–4: **Operating Income/Expenses Worksheet**

► Get With the Plan

Regardless of how well you think you know your business, you need a written business plan. Writing your plans down forces you to think them through and gives you a chance to examine them for consistency and thoroughness.

If you're excited about your business, creating a business plan should be an exciting process. It will help you define and evaluate the overall feasibility of your concept, clarify your goals, and determine what you'll need for startup and long-term operations.

This is a living, breathing document that will provide you with a road map for your company. You'll use it as a guide, referring to it regularly as you work through the startup process and then during the operation of your business. And if you're going to be seeking outside financing, either in the form of loans or investors, your business plan will be the tool that convinces funding sources of the worthiness of your venture. Look for tools and resources for creating a business plan in the Appendix.

Locating Your Business

As we've said many times, one of the great perks of running a medical billing service is that it lends itself ideally to the homebased entrepreneur. It doesn't require a high-traffic or high-visibility location and doesn't need to be in the trendy part of town or in an industrial complex, although those are certainly options. You don't need a mahogany-paneled office with a lobby and conference room to impress or entertain clients. The only space requirement is an area large enough for your desk, your chair, a few filing cabinets, and perhaps a bookshelf.

It's convenient—you couldn't get any closer to your office unless you slept with your computer. It's economical—you don't need to spend money on leased space, extra utilities, transportation costs, or lunches down at the corner grill.

Working at home is not, however, mandatory. You may want to leave your laundry, your dog, and/or your kids/spouse at home while you go off to an office space that's nice, quiet, clean, and yours alone.

The Home Office

If you choose to be homebased, you can locate your office work space anywhere in the house that's convenient. Most homebased MIBs have a dedicated office that's reserved just for the business. You could locate your home office in a den, a FROG (finished room over garage), the garage itself, the recreational vehicle parked in the backyard (so long as you run electrical and phone lines out to it), or a corner of the kitchen. Keep in mind that whatever space you choose will be your workstation and command center. If you have a boisterous family, a cubbyhole in your bedroom might be much more conducive to quiet, clear thinking than a nook in the den with the big-screen TV blaring at all hours. Also remember that yelling into the phone over cartoon kerblams and pows will not make you sound particularly professional to your clients.

The Tax Man Speaketh

Another advantage to the home office is the ability to write it off as a home business. The IRS will graciously allow you to deduct money from your income taxes if you're using a portion of your home as your income-producing work space. You can deduct a percentage of expenses equivalent to the percentage of space your home office occupies. If, for example, you're using one room in an eight-room house, you can deduct one-eighth of your rent or mortgage payment plus one-eighth of your utility bills off your taxes. You can also deduct based on the square footage used for business out of the total of your house or apartment.

There is, of course, an *if* involved here. You can use this deduction if you're using this space solely as your office. If you've turned your spare bedroom into your office and you don't use it for anything but conducting your business, then you qualify. If, however, your office is tucked into a corner of the kitchen and you're still feeding people in there, you do not qualify for the home office deduction (unless you can convince the IRS that you order Chinese every night and the refrigerator is actually a file cabinet).

Growing Pains

As your business grows, you may find that your dedicated office has become a dedicated house—and that it's time to move up to commercial office space. Because the medical billing service doesn't rely on client traffic or a prestigious address, any area that appeals to you and your pocketbook is up for grabs. It's a good idea to look into an inexpensive office space, off the pricier main drag. Even better is the second or third floor of a commercial building such as a bank or insurance company. These buildings always have space available and are less expensive than space in a high-traffic retail area, which is perfect because you don't need high visibility anyway.

> **tip** ⓘ
>
> Even if your homebased office does not qualify for the home office deduction, you can still deduct other expenses—inventory, storage, equipment, shipping, automobile, marketing, etc., that are legitimate costs of doing business.

Let's Make a Deal

Locating that gem of an office requires as much as ingenuity and forethought as researching your market. But a little chutzpah pays off.

When the Walnut Creek MIB started her business, she wanted to locate in a commercial space. "I knew the landlord of this building and that it was underoccupied," she says. "It was a great, quiet location that I thoroughly enjoyed. We had a park out of one set of windows and a church out of the other one. It was just very peaceful there.

"So I went and talked to him and told him what I was trying to do and negotiated an excellent rent. He always said that he lost money on me being there. I signed a lease for three years with great hope and all fingers crossed. He was fabulous. Even after that lease ran out, he still gave me an excellent rent. I had started out with just one suite, but when we expanded I ended up with three. So I was a pretty good bet for him."

Don't be afraid to negotiate. Like the Walnut Creek MIB, you just might end up with the deal of a lifetime. Be honest. Let the prospective landlord know what you can afford. Offer your best bet. If he doesn't go for it, ask what concessions he can make. If you can't come to an agreement, thank him for his time and bid him a fond farewell. There are plenty of other office spaces in the sea.

Alternative Officing

If commercial office space is not your bag, you might consider a more unconventional approach. Rent a house or an apartment (providing you check the zoning laws first). This may present an advantage over an office suite because of the private kitchen and bathroom. If you already live in an apartment, you may choose to rent another unit in the same building to use as your office. You can walk to work. And the landlord may give you a package deal—or a finder's fee!

Take a space over a storefront downtown. How about over a coffeehouse or doughnut shop or bagel bakery? What better incentive to get to work in the morning!

Or strike up a deal with a doctor. You bill a certain amount of work for him in exchange for office space. This arrangement might especially appeal to a physician who's just starting out in business himself.

aha!

Tap your local commercial real estate broker for info and advice. Besides giving you the rental lowdown in your town, he can act as a terrific referral for potential clients for you. A good realtor knows everybody in town and usually has a stable of doctors as his own clients.

The Medical Complex

The medical complex is the high-rent district. But don't bypass the high-density doctor zone without a thought. Get creative. Try negotiating with the leasing agent, especially if you can find a new complex. Point out that your business can be a draw for doctors considering the suites.

The major draw for you to locate in a medical complex is, of course, convenience, both for your clients and for yourself. This is especially true if you are going to be doing

▶ How Suite It Is

Not crazy about leasing commercial space, but can't work out of your home? An office option to consider is an executive suite, where you have your own private space, and the landlord provides receptionist and secretarial services, faxing, photocopying, conference rooms, and other support services as part of the package. Executive suites can help you project the image of a professional operation at a more affordable cost than a traditional office, and they can be found in most commercial office areas. Shop around, and be sure to talk with existing tenants to be sure they're happy before signing a lease.

full-practice management. When patients visit the doctor, you will be readily available to answer questions, get insurance precertification, or field complaints.

Doctors and their staff will have easy access to you and your office. They won't have to fax or mail superbills or patient information, plus they can sneak over for a cup of java and a sympathetic ear when the patient crush gets too traumatic.

On the plus side for you, you don't have to drive to pick up billing materials, and as new doctors come on the scene, you'll already be there as the answer to their billing prayers. On the negative side, you'll have commuter woes, the added expense of a lease and all those meal decisions—sack lunch, corner café, or takeout.

As a side note, be sure to check and see if any competitors are located nearby. If a medical claims billing competitor is down the hall it's going to make your marketing job tougher, so look elsewhere.

The Outside Office

If you plan to set up your office in a commercial location, you'll want to think about visitors. In this case, your bricks-and-2 x 4s bookcase and the milk-crate filing cabinet from college are not your best option. You'll want "real" office furniture that conveys the impression of clean, quiet efficiency. It doesn't need to be fancy, but it should be pleasant and comfortable.

Your visitors will, for the most part, be on the run, but you can provide a chair or two on which to alight. You'll also want that American office altarpiece, the coffee maker, and if you can provide a tidbit or two—home-baked cookies or a jar of candies—you'll probably have friends for life. Doctors' staffs are on the run as much as waitresses, and high-energy perks can be a boon.

Of course, even if your office is in your home doesn't mean you can't still have coffee and cookies. Goodies are as close as your kitchen. And so are all the other joys of home. After all, isn't that one of the great perks of having a home office?

It is according to the MIB in Denver. She relocated her office from a commercial space to her home so that, she says, "I could be here with my children and keep track of everybody and everything."

aha!

If your closet is of the sliding-doors/runs-along-one-wall variety, take out the clothes and stash them somewhere else. Remove the doors, and you have a dandy office nook.

Portrait of a Home Office

If you opt for the home office, it's important to remember that you are still a professional. Your work quarters—like you—should be organized and efficient. If at all possible,

► First Impressions

Even if your office is in your garage, your business still needs a professional image. But instead of worrying about the right shade of charcoal for your clients' chairs, arranging the seating for that just-right aura of subliminal authority, or choosing signed lithographs for the walls, you can create your professional image through your business cards, stationery, and logo.

You can do it all yourself with desktop publishing. But, as with deciding on a business name, be sure that the image you're beaming into the minds of prospects and clients is the one you want. Leave the over-the-top-trendy or oh-so-cutesy images for other businesses. A logo featuring dancing skeletons with mariachis won't quite cut it, and unless you're specializing in pediatrics and pediatrics alone, a cuddly teddy bear is not the best logo, either.

Your most important goal with your printed materials is to convey the impression of brisk, organized efficiency and expertise. This is what you're selling. Have a friend or family member look over your designs before you commit to a print run of 500 cards or letterhead. Do they see typos? Amateurishness? Or do they catch the gleam of a business riding the waves of proficiency?

designate a separate room with four walls and a door. Aim for pleasant, quiet, well-lit surroundings. You're going to be spending a lot of time in this space, so you want it to be comfortable.

If you can't carve out a dedicated space, by all means take over a corner of another room. But consider it your permanent office. Clearing your work materials off the dining room table before every meal is a definite drag.

Appropriate a desk or table large enough to hold your computer, keyboard, phone, and pencil holder, stapler, etc., and still have enough room to spread out your working papers. A charming 19th-century cherry-wood secretary looks great but probably will not allow enough space for several stacks of files plus you and your computer. Don't skimp on elbow room.

Commandeer a comfortable chair, one that fits under the desk with enough legroom for you to stretch out. Make it as cushy as possible. Your posterior and the

aha!

Don't come out of the closet—go into it! Some homes, especially older ones, have walk-in closets—some with windows—that are large enough to turn into a cozy little office. Just make sure yours has adequate ventilation and light.

seat of that chair are going to be in close contact for many, many hours, and a sturdy kitchen chair is going to feel like concrete in short order.

You should have a file cabinet or two with locks so they are HIPAA-compliant. For everyday filing, you can get by with a set of cardboard file boxes. Place them close at hand but not underfoot. It's no fun digging through the back of the clothes closet or running out to the garage every time somebody calls with a question. You should also have a bookcase or shelf to hold your reference library. Again, make it as convenient as possible. Use the handy worksheet in Figure 7–1 to locate and design your home office.

Make Yourself at Home

List three possible locations in your home:

1. _____

2. _____

3. _____

Make a physical survey of each location.

❑ Are phone and electrical outlets placed so that your equipment can easily access them? Or will you be faced with unsightly, unsafe cords snaking across the carpet?

❑ Will your current desk or table or the one you have your eye on fit? Measure your space carefully to be sure.

❑ Do you have adequate lighting? If not, can you create or import it?

❑ Is there proper ventilation?

❑ What is the noise factor?

❑ Is there room to spread out your work?

Optional:

❑ How close is it to the coffee maker? Refrigerator? (This can be either a plus or minus, depending on your current waistline and jitter factor.)

FIGURE 7–1: **Design Your Home Office Worksheet**

Employees, Insurance, and Other Facts of Life

D epending on how much growth you envision for your business, you may never need employees. Or you may expand to the point where you can't do everything yourself. Employees are another of those funny facts of life that seem to bring with them as many cons as pros. When you hire help, you are not a swinging single anymore. You have responsibilities.

Suddenly there's payroll to be met, workers' compensation insurance to be paid, state and federal employee taxes to be paid. And work to be delegated.

Some people are born employers, finding it easy to teach someone else the ropes and then hand over the reins. Others never feel quite comfortable telling someone else what to do or how to do it.

"At one point," says the Denver MIB, "I had a staff of about seven. I felt that I had lost control of really doing the work that I love to do, and I was managing people. I grew more than I really felt comfortable growing, so I scaled it back down, and now it's just myself and my daughter. It's just the two of us.

"We've moved back into my home. I did have an office space. I downsized. This is how I want to do it, out of my home so that I can work any time I want to and I can do the work myself instead of managing people all day. I guess I'm a control freak. [I] want to keep control of [the business] and want to know what's going on. And I really enjoy doing the work."

Hired Hands

If you're not fortunate enough to have live-in help, you may want to consider hiring an assistant.

Mary V. and her former partner had one full-time employee, whom they took on after three years in business. This employee did a good portion of their data entry, although she did not come on board with a background in medical billing. "What you need more than anything," Mary explains, "is attention to detail."

Since your assistant will function as an extension of yourself and will represent your business to the outside world, you'll want to choose carefully. A background in data entry or medical billing, or even medical assisting or nursing, is certainly a plus, but just as important— if not more so—is trainability. A person who has no knowledge at all of computers is liable to take an enormous chunk of valuable time to train, but a person who knows computers but not specifically medical billing can be taught to do things exactly the way you want them done.

Organization is a must. So are good telephone skills and the ability to think independently. Your employee

> **tip** ⓘ
>
> Every prospective employee should fill out an application—even if it's someone you know, and even if they have submitted a detailed resume. A resume is not a signed, sworn statement acknowledging that you can fire them if they lie; an application is.

will be dealing with clients, insurers, and patients. He or she must be polite, accurate, and assertive. She should be able to bring problems to your attention but also be able to solve problems on her own. If she is constantly interrupting you with questions, you might as well handle everything yourself.

Pay rates for a good data entry clerk run from about $10 to $18 per hour, although this can vary from region to region and on the level of experience. The Walnut Creek MIB pays her employees, all medical billing specialists, $12 and up.

Hours are up to you. You can hire someone to work part time, say, four hours a morning or afternoon or two or three days a week, or you can use your assistant full time, depending on your needs.

As the workload grows and you need a full-time person or need to extend the hours, either change the status of your part-time employee, or if that won't work, be creative: Consider hiring a second part-timer or come up with some other solution that lets you retain a valuable person and still get the work done. Flexibility is the key to finding and keeping good employees.

Administrative Assistant/Medical Billing

Full-Time Employment

Hours: 8 A.M. to 5 P.M.

Duties: Responsible for the overall daily operations of a busy medical claims billing office. Responsibilities include answering phones; communicating with patients, doctors' offices, and insurance companies; patient data entry, verification of insurance eligibility and benefits, insurance authorizations, and pre-certification; filing paper and electronic claims; assistance with appealing claims.

Qualifications: Have office administrative experience; experienced with CPT and ICD coding; possess knowledge of EHR, Microsoft Office, and HIPPA compliance; familiar with medical terminology. Data entry skills a plus; excellent customer service skills a must.

Send resume to: Needa Worker, 1234 E. 53rd St., Somewhere, CA 00000

FIGURE 8–1: **Sample Help Wanted Notice**

▶ The Backup Brain

Hiring an employee is one of those take-a-deep-breath-or-hyperventilate steps. You're taking on an extension of yourself, someone who with any luck will become not just another pair of hands but a backup brain, a friend, ally, and member of your business family. How do you choose someone to fill all of those shoes?

You want someone with the following skills and abilities:

- ▶ *Analytical skills.* Can they think a problem through and arrive at a solution?

- ▶ *Oral communication skills.* Do they have a good phone personality? Can they communicate a problem? Resolve that problem? Is their vocabulary good? Grammar?

- ▶ *Written communication skills.* Can they write an effective patient or insurance response letter, explaining the problem? Detail the resolution? Communicate grammatically? Punctuate properly?

- ▶ *Detail-oriented.* Can they enter correct codes and patient information without transposing or scrambling?

- ▶ *Able to take direction.* Can they follow directions? And can they do so without getting insulted or defensive?

- ▶ *Personality complements your own.* Some people work better with cheery chatterboxes; others go for the strong, silent type. If you are one and your prospective assistant is another, think twice.

Slave Labor

An alternative to hiring an employee is to shanghai an unsuspecting family member. The New Jersey MIB sets her husband to work on occasion while the Denver MIB puts her four daughters, ages 17 to 23, in the computer operator's seat. The eldest is a true employee who's earned the title of bookkeeper; the others fill in here and there. This "helping out" strategy has the advantage of no employee taxes or insurance, although—at least in the case of teens—you'll probably still have to pay your workers. This way, your help is on call 24 hours a day, and you'll know if they're really sick or if they've gone fishin'.

tip

If your local community college offers courses in medical billing or front-office medical assisting, check with its job bank. Students learning the very skills you need can be a terrific employment source.

Since much of the data entry can be done at any time, your family crew members can work after school, on a Saturday afternoon, or just about any time that fits into their schedules. Helping mom or dad or a spouse with the family business gives everybody a warm fuzzy feeling of pitching in and can be a great togetherness booster.

"And hopefully," the Denver biller says, "they will all take over and then I can retire and just sit back and watch."

Yet another employment alternative is farming out your overload. You can subcontract your data entry work to another billing service and then pay either hourly or per claim. One MIB envisions a time when other people could be routinely set up to do medical billing in their own homes as satellites of his business, thus helping others as he helps himself.

The Temp

Temporary employment services offer the option of employees you can use like library books, borrowing them for the time you need them and then "returning" them with no hard feelings. These employees come prescreened, and all insurance and taxes are covered by the agency. The drawback to the temporary employee is expense.

"I did like the person they sent me very much," the Denver MIB says of her ventures into hiring a temporary bookkeeper and file clerk, "but they're extremely expensive to use. I felt I probably could have gotten someone just as capable by doing a want ad. I probably would have needed to train to some extent, but I wouldn't have had to use that middleman and have the extra expense I incurred."

Insuring Your Gems

Once you find those gems of employees, you'll need to think about caring for them. Workers' compensation insurance laws vary from state to state; check with your insurance agent for details in your area. Workers' comp covers you for any illness or injury that might occur, from a paper cut gone septic to a back injury from lifting heavy file boxes to permanent computer eyestrain. (People can come up with a lot of strange complaints when money's involved.)

aha!

Give your employees perks for production. "I just switched [my employee daughter] to commission because I charge the physicians a percentage of what we collect," the Denver MIB says. "I want her to have an incentive to collect more for the physicians, so I give her a percentage of what we collect. So she basically can write her own paycheck by how much she wants to work and how much she can bring in."

tip

When you contract out work, you gain a valuable networking ally. This person will in turn contract work to you or refer people to you.

Although your employee may be working in your home, your homeowners' insurance might not pay for any such problem on the grounds that it's actually a workers' compensation case.

Rather than making yourself a nervous wreck (incurring your own mental health claim) over all this, check with your insurance agent and then make an informed decision.

"Initially I did the workers' comp month to month," the Walnut Creek MIB says, "because I couldn't afford to pay a whole chunk at a time. They were pretty understanding about that. I worked with The Hartford Company (formerly ITT Hartford), and they were great. You can do it [that way] when you're in a pinch. I had to have it, but I didn't want to take all my funds and pay a whole year at a time. They worked out a payment arrangement with me. It cost a little bit [in] finance charges, but I think it was only a few bucks a month, something like that."

You might want to consider health benefits for your staff. "I provided my staff with health insurance initially and a small life insurance policy," she explains, "and now we have expanded to health, dental, vision, and life insurance."

And they don't even have to handle the paperwork. "The physicians we go to do the claim billing," the former nurse says, "so we're not even involved with that. Which is kind of strange."

The Error of Omitting

Some MIBs are concerned with errors and omissions insurance, which is somewhat similar to malpractice insurance and covers you for nightmarish possibilities such as having a client sue you.

Insurers charge according to risk. Errors and omissions coverage for an MIB business should be about $1,000 to $5,000 per year, but be sure to check with your personal insurance agent for details.

As long as you're worrying at the insurance bone, be sure to update your homeowners' or office rental policy for all your equipment, especially anything new you purchase.

"A lot of insurance companies won't tell you this," the New Jersey MIB confides, "but you can get a nice discount if you send in a digital recording of your office equipment

aha!

A payroll service, which computes and pays employee taxes on your behalf for a minimal fee, can be a boon. Check it out!

▶ The Test

OK, your prospective employee looks sharp, sounds professional, and has a nice resume. But how can you know how he'll actually perform once he's on the job? Test him out!

▶ *Write out a typical scenario in which a claim has been denied for a fairly simple reason.* (You be the judge.) You might, for example, use a case in which surgery is shown before the pre-op exam or discharge date before the admission. Ask your prospect to solve the problem.

▶ *Present a scenario of a patient who hasn't paid his bill.* Ask your prospect what he'd say over the phone. Have him type out a letter requesting payment.

▶ *If your prospect is familiar with medical billing, have him enter a claim.* How does he do?

▶ *Have him enter a column of numbers on a calculator.* Does he add it up quickly and correctly?

After you've done all of this for each prospect, you'll want to read resumes, check references, and then use your own people skills. How do you feel intuitively about them?

---

inventory. I ended up getting an annual 10 percent break. Any time I buy something, I update that recording and send it over to them. Anything happens, I'll get full value."

As with everything else in the MIB business, it pays to get creative. And don't forget that your insurance agent is a great source for new clients!

Forward to the Basics

If you and your computer are starting out from square one, you won't want to concern yourself with insurance policy perks. You can always add these on later when you build a staff and the funds to support them.

Starting out small, or keeping your business small, is in itself a perk, as the Denver MIB found out. She has a young son at home, along with her four daughters. "All he likes to do is turn off the computers," she says. "I haven't taught him anything else right yet. But that's the importance. I think he's the main reason I like to keep it at home—to have him here with me. I love what I do."

Make sure you have the business insurance bases covered: Consider picking up Entrepreneur's *Start Your Own Business, Sixth Edition: The Only Startup Book You'll Ever Need* for complete information on all small business needs.

Equipping Your Business

Y our office will be your operating theater—
the dramatic heart of your business—and the
proper equipment will contribute greatly to your
success. Just as you wouldn't want your neurologist performing brain surgery with a chain saw, so it goes that you
won't want to perform delicate electronic operations with a
clunker of a computer.

We've provided a handy checklist (see Figure 9–1, page 137) to help you determine what you will need, what you already have on hand, and which of those in-stock items is MIB-ready. It's been designed with the one-person home office in mind. If you have partners or employees or you just inherited a million dollars from a mysterious foundation with the stipulation that you spend at least half on office equipment, you might want to make modifications. Die-hard shoppers might want to rush out and buy every item brand-spanking new, but this might not be necessary. Some or all of these things might already be meandering around your home, just waiting to be put to use. After you have read this chapter, run through the checklist and evaluate your stock. Is your computer MIB-ready, or is it an antique that won't be able to keep up the pace? Does your answering machine take and receive clearly audible messages, or does it tend to garble crucial information? How about that printer? Can it produce professional-looking materials in short order, or does it take ages to spit out a solitary, quavery page? Now, checklist in hand, let's take a whirlwind virtual shopping spree. Ready, steady, go!

Wait a second. Let's discuss something first. There's always the buy of a lifetime and there's always the ultimate fancy-schmancy tip-top of the line. What we're looking for here are the lower-end and middle-of-the-road models.

Computer Glitterati

Your computer will be the star of your office setup, coordinating your billing, accounting, word-processing, and desktop publishing activities. In addition to your billing software, it will be arguably your most important purchase. If you already own a computer, you'll want to make sure it's capable of handling the tasks it will be given.

You will want your new computer to have the most current version of Windows since this is what new MIB software packages are geared for. To run your medical billing software properly, you'll need at least 2 GB memory (preferably 8 GB), plus at least a 250 GB hard drive, a DVD-ROM drive, and a modem with wireless router, wifi capability, and high-speed internet connection.

You can expect to pay from $1,000 to $2,500 for a good name-brand computer, with prices increasing as you add on goodies.

Monitoring the Monitor

Monitors frequently come as part of the computer package, but they can be bought separately. Make sure you get an LED widescreen monitor with a 19-inch screen—large enough to make long-term viewing comfortable.

The MIB Office Checklist

❑ Windows-based computer with LED monitor and DVD-ROM drive $_____

❑ Laser or inkjet printer   _____

❑ Fax machine   _____

❑ Business/marketing software:

    Word processing   _____

    Desktop publishing   _____

    Accounting   _____

❑ Phones, two to three lines with voice mail, or answering machine   _____

❑ Internet service   _____

❑ Uninterruptible power supply   _____

❑ Flash or external hard drive   _____

❑ Surge protector   _____

❑ Calculator   _____

❑ Computer/copier/fax paper   _____

❑ Blank business cards   _____

❑ Blank letterhead stationery   _____

❑ Matching envelopes   _____

❑ 10 x 13 envelopes   _____

❑ Legal-sized envelopes for mailing claims   _____

❑ Return address self-stamper or stickers   _____

❑ Extra printer cartridge   _____

❑ Extra fax/toner cartridge   _____

❑ Mouse pad   _____

❑ Miscellaneous office supplies (pencils, paper clips, etc.)   _____

Not on the Critical List

❑ Copier   _____

❑ Desk   _____

❑ Desk chair   _____

❑ Filing cabinet   _____

❑ Bookcase   _____

Total Office Equipment and Furniture Expenditures $_____

FIGURE 9–1: **The MIB Office Checklist**

▶ Cybersense

It's easy to get wowed—and wooed—by all the computers at the store vying for your attention. Here's the professional take on what to buy from Margaret, a business machines specialist with Office Depot in Panama City, Florida.

Sit back and take a long, hard look, Margaret counsels, before you purchase a new computer. Her rule of thumb for a small MIB-type business is to consider spending between $200 and $500 a year on your computer system. For example, if you spend $2,000 on a system (computer, monitor, and printer), you should figure on keeping it for four to five years. If that system helps you make money, she says, then when it comes time to sell, upgrade, or give it to the kids, it's lived a useful life.

Margaret also cautions that people tend to overspend. They want to buy the best and brightest but unfortunately frequently end up using only 50 percent of their system's capabilities. She suggests starting out small. "For the entrepreneur or supplemental income [buyer], there's no need to overspend." You can get a good system for around $1,000 to $2,000.

Keep in mind that as an MIB you'll spend a lot of time in front of that monitor—this is one place where bigger is definitely better. A few extra dollars spent upfront will save hours of squinting in the long haul. If you purchase your monitor separately, you can expect to dish out less than $200 for a 19-inch model.

Flashy Drives

Data management is the lifeblood of your MIB business, so you'll want to back up your files on a daily basis. A flash drive—a small memory stick device with storage capacities of 2 GB to 128 GB—is one of several efficient ways to make these backup chores zip right along. Prices range from $10 to $70.

However, if you have a large amount of data to back up, an external hard drive would be the most convenient method because of how quickly they can copy the data and the amount of storage they can hold: 80 GB to 2 TB (1 terabyte is equal to 1,024 GB). These lightweight, portable gadgets generally run from $100 to $500.

Purring Printers

A good printer is a must, even though much of your billing will be done online. You'll want to produce reports, charts, graphs, brochures, newsletters, thank-you letters, pay-up-or-else letters, contracts, statements, and sundry other materials, and they all need to look polished and professional. The materials you produce will be a direct reflection on your company. If you still have a dot-matrix printer, ditch it now. Faint, shaky dot-matrix correspondence looks amateurish. Sharp, bold graphics and print give your business an aura of confidence and success.

You also want a printer that's fast. There's nothing quite like the frustration of waiting for material to trickle out of a slow-going printer. One page per minute can seem like one page per hour.

Fortunately, really hot-stuff printers are much less expensive now than ever before. You can purchase a laser or an inkjet, many of which can produce all the wonderful colors of commercial artwork. Color-capable

> **tip** ⓘ
>
> An increasingly popular way to backup critical files is heading for the "clouds"—meaning online backup services. These cost-effective solutions enable you to automatically and securely store your data offsite for a single computer or the entire office. (See the Appendix for recommendations.)

models print more slowly than their black-and-white colleagues, but if you'll be doing lots of marketing materials like brochures and newsletters, then you'll want to consider color. You can expect to pay as little as $100 to as much as $1,000 for a color inkjet or laser printer suitable for business purposes.

The Fax for You

A fax machine, as we've discussed, is a good way to get raw billing materials from your doctors. But more than that, it makes life much breezier when you want to send or receive certain kinds of information in a flash. For example, you might want to send the insurance carrier a piece of documentation right after you've spoken with them—before they forget what the conversation was about. Ditto for a document to a doctor or patient for clarification. And then, of course, there's that lunch order to the deli down the street.

Fax machines can be purchased as combo fax/copiers, printers, and scanners. They can be very slow when used as a printer, so be sure to check before you buy. Also, make sure the fax machine you purchase will print on plain paper. Expect to pay as little as $100 for a basic plain-paper model and up to $900 for the multifunction jobbies.

Soft on Software

As we've said before, your software is going to be your closest partner after your significant other, so choose carefully. The list of suitors is lengthy, with medical billing/patient accounting programs and packages ranging from $500 to $5,000. Different packages have different capabilities, but more expensive is not necessarily better or worse. You can buy the bare-bones software or purchase a complete business opportunity package, which can include lead generation, seminars, marketing help, and hold-your-hand technical support along with the software.

Some of the medical claims business opportunities you may come across will seem quite lucrative and dazzling; however, look at them carefully before committing to make sure you're getting your money's worth. Consider that hiring a local marketing specialist generally costs a lot less and will give you personalized attention.

Whichever option you choose, you'll want to make sure the software is the suitor of your dreams. Here are your dream date must-haves:

- ▶ Fields for patient and insurance information
- ▶ Ability to establish CPT and ICD-10 databases for your doctors' specialties
- ▶ Electronic claims capability
- ▶ Paper claims capability
- ▶ Posting of payments to patient accounts using open-item accounting, which applies payments toward specific charges rather than toward the patient's total balance
- ▶ Ability to format and print claim forms and patient statements
- ▶ Ability to format patient, provider, insurance company, and other custom lists
- ▶ Ability to generate and print reports, including patient ledgers, aging of accounts receivable by patient and insurance carrier, practice analysis (breakdown of charges, income and adjustments for the provider's practice), and other customized reports
- ▶ User-friendliness
- ▶ Provides training and support
- ▶ Complete documentation
- ▶ Readily available coding updates
- ▶ HIPAA-compliant for electronic health records
- ▶ Secure backup of data files
- ▶ Remote access (optional)

You will also want to consider if you would prefer software that is PC-based or accessed online. PC-based is good for someone with a small practice if the hardware upgrades are minimal; the same goes for online if you don't want to worry about backing up your data and software maintenance. However, if you have several employees at one location like our Napa MIB, a separate dedicated server may work better.

Once you identify the software of your dreams and pocketbook, make sure it has a good reputation. Find out how long the vendor or developer has been in business and how many people (preferably thousands) are using the product. Get references, and don't be shy about calling them. Most MIBs are only too happy to share their experiences and will be glad to give you tips other than just a software reference. It can be one of your first forays into networking.

The Minnesota MIB says that the software you choose should have good health-records management. "I would recommend doing online research and find the program that fits your needs based on the type of billing you will be doing: medical, dental, Medicaid, Medicare, etc."

Ask lots of questions when doing your research. Is the program user-friendly? How good is the technical

warning ⚠

Many successful billing services have run into rough water when their software vendor went out of business, leaving them with no source for future updates or additional training. Do your homework. Find out all you can.

▶ Get Your Head in the Clouds

When reviewing electronic health records software you will need to think about what key functions you need it to do (no, they don't make coffee), as well as whether to go with software or a cloud-based system. The first is cost and understanding that cheaper is not necessarily better. The second is automated coding that will take information from the EHR by way of keywords and make superbills an electronic process. Finally, the ability to keep track of payments, denial trends, and money enables billers to identify CPTs.

With a cloud-based EHR, there is no software or hardware to download and subsequently manage. Instead, the information is always up to date, which keeps errors low across the changing medical landscape. Computer-installed software also automatically generates the codes, using clinical terms and concepts to help find keywords and attach the right code. However, if the software hasn't been routinely updated, the procedure codes might bypass the newest edits in the event that a code has been flagged for National Correct Coding Initiatives (NCCI) compliance.

Last, but not least, the Georgia MIB says a biller/coder needs to know how to read an electronic health record. "That seems so elementary to say that, but it's true," says Marsha S. "Every system has their own spin on things and each user within an EHR system is going to have their uniqueness about how they enter things. Make sure the record is complete before the provider locks the note and that all the information is correct. If it's not complete or includes errors, it will negatively impact your billing and reimbursement."

support? How available is the technical support? How long has the person you're talking to been using the program? Are they happy with it? Have they heard any rumbles about possible problems in the future, such as the vendor leaving for a permanent Tahitian vacation?

More Software

A dazzling array of software lines the shelves of most office supply stores, ready to help you perform every business task—design and print your own checks, develop professional-quality marketing materials, make mailing lists and labels, be your own attorney and accountant.

Most new computers come preloaded with all the software you'll need for basic office procedures. If yours doesn't or if you've lucked into a stripped-down hand-me-down, you might want to look into the following programs. You should have a word-processing program to write correspondence, contracts, reports to go with the charts from your billing software, and whatever else strikes your fancy. You can find a good basic program such as Microsoft Word (the business industry standard) for $100 or Corel WordPerfect Office for around $260.

You might also want an accounting program such as Intuit's QuickBooks or Quicken to track your business finances. These are a sort of checkbook on your computer that make record-keeping a breeze. The program can be downloaded online or purchased on a CD-ROM. You assign categories such as office supplies and business travel to the checks you write, and at tax time, you print out a report showing how much money you spent for what. Your accountant not only will thank you but will charge you less for not having to wade through all your receipts. You can expect to pay from $59 to $250 for your cyberspace checkbook.

You'll want a desktop publishing program for those polished marketing materials. Try Broderbund's Print Shop Pro Publisher Deluxe for around $100 or Microsoft Publisher for $150. Both are very user-friendly and can be used to create a bevy of marketing materials from business cards and brochures to banners and signage. A nice complement is Photoshop Elements from Adobe, a slimmed-down version of the big daddy of photography/design software, Photoshop. For about $100, you get most major elements of the straight-up version, but with more flexibility and ease of use. It's a great graphics programs for beginners.

The Business Opportunity

Shopping for the right software, clearinghouse, or business opportunity is a lot like going on a blind date. You know you're going to have to run through a certain number of nerds

warning

Is a business opportunity seller doing the hustle? Watch out for a salesperson who says things like "Territories are going fast." Legitimate sellers will not pressure you to rush into a big decision. If someone does, just say no.

before you find the one that makes your heart sing and your computer soar. This is not to say that nine out of ten vendors (and by "vendors" we mean software and business opportunities) are duds. Like other loves in your life, what one person considers perfect may leave another flat.

There are a number of potential business opportunities available for a medical claims billing services with prices starting as low as $1,000 and running more than $7,500, depending on what perks are included such as type of software, training, online and/or phone support, and number of users. Some of the more popular companies are:

▶ *MediPro.* MediPro has been offering medical billing software since 1989 and is highly respected in the industry, with prices starting at $3,500 for a single user. For more information, go to: www.medipro.com.

▶ *Collaborate MD.* This is another popular choice due to its automated billing processes that help to streamline billing and coding functions. Its user-friendly software starts at $165 per month. Additional fees include claim processing, provider usage fees, and other incidentals. Go to: www.collaboratemd.com for more information.

▶ *Office Ally.* Recommended by the Napa MIB, this has a complete arsenal of web-based solutions including a clearinghouse, electronic health records, customized superbills, claims and revenue tracking, and much more. Some of their features are free; others start with a $30 monthly fee. Visit http://cms.officeally.com for more information.

▶ *Franchising Opportunities.* Franchising can be a great way to start a new business because even though you are in business for yourself, you're not alone. You can start your new venture with a proven working model, an enthusiastic team of

warning

Not all business opportunities are the same. One might consist of as little as a startup manual; another will provide you with software, in-depth training, and ongoing sales, marketing, and technical support. It is your responsibility—a big one—to find out exactly what you're buying. Don't make the assumption that because one offers a particular service or feature, another one will, too.

go-getters, and comprehensive hands-on training. However, you will need capital to get started. Examples are ClaimTek Systems that requires a minimum of $20,000 and American Business Systems which has an initial investment of $25,000 (see the Appendix).

Before investing in any type of medical billing business opportunity be sure to check and see if any complaints have been filed against them with the Better Business Bureau, your state's attorney general's office and the consumer protection agency in your area. Ask for references and then verify them.

Clearinghouse Check-Up

The Minnesota MIB says that clearinghouses can be your best friend or your worst nightmare. So, before you decide on a clearinghouse, don your mental detective garb and investigate. Make sure you find the answers to the following:

▶ Which payers is the system connected to? Does it handle all major commercial payers? How about HMOs, the Blues, Medicare, and Medicaid?

▶ How many payers does it connect to? The more it hooks up with, the less additional work for you.

▶ Can you rely on it to accommodate all payer reporting requirements?

▶ How many medical practices and billing services does it count as clients? A large number here is a good indicator that the service is tops.

▶ Does the clearinghouse return claim audit information to you in the form of reports? How long does it take to receive information? Some return information in a few minutes, some in 24 hours, others in a few days.

▶ Does the clearinghouse offer value-added services to help improve your productivity, such as electronic remittance advisories, electronic funds transfers, or suspense files?

▶ What equipment, software, and training will you need?

▶ What kind of ongoing support is offered? This is a biggie. Since payers frequently change the score card, buying each other out and potentially changing data requirements, the system must be periodically updated.

▶ What's the track record for support and maintenance? How fast will the clearinghouse respond if you have a problem?

▶ References? Ask for names and phone numbers of current clients and then do your homework. Check them out. If any are near you, ask if you can drop by and see the system in action.

▶ How long has the clearinghouse been in business? Check around for any rumors of disbanding or dissatisfaction.

▶ Are the system and software fully functional? Purchasing a system under development can spell trouble.

▶ Can the system accommodate your billing software?

▶ What's the per-claim cost?

▶ Is there an annual fee?

▶ Is there a per-doctor fee?

▶ Will it send paper claims to payers that aren't EDI-capable? This is another biggie. If it does, it streamlines your work considerably.

▶ Who has access to the data you submit? What security safeguards are in place to protect confidential information?

Marsha S., the Georgia MIB, says it is important for a clearinghouse to have a great support system and to be able to do enrollment for electronic filing for insurance companies. "I would look for one that has EFT as well; that way you can send claims and download EOBs all in one place."

You can expect to pay from zero to $300 in clearinghouse initiation fees. In addition, some clearinghouses may charge a per-doctor fee of $50 or more.

▶ Step into My Office

Office furniture is another optional item. It's important that your work environment is comfortable and ergonomic, but if you're homebased, it's perfectly acceptable to start off with an old door set on cinder blocks for a desk and a milk crate for your files. When you're ready to go the big step toward real office furniture for that oh-so-professional look, you have a stunning array of possibilities to choose from.

We shopped the big office-supply warehouse stores and found midrange desks from $150 to $400; a computer work center for $250; printer stands from $70 to $90; two-drawer, letter-size file cabinets (which can double as your printer stand) from $50 to $200; and a four-shelf bookcase for $100.

Chairs are a very personal matter. Some people like the dainty secretary's chair for its economy of space; others want the tonier high-back executive model. There are chairs with kangaroo pockets and chairs with pneumatic height adjustments. Prices range from $60 to $150 on up.

Hello, Central

Chances are you will probably have two to three telephone lines coming into your home office. Therefore, you will want a two-line phone so you can put one on hold while you are answering the other line. You can divide up the lines any way you like: You might put your home line and your business line on the two-line phone, leaving the third line for your fax machine. Or you might put the business and fax line on the two-line phone, leaving your home line in the kitchen or den. Perhaps you wish to use a mobile phone as your main office number, freeing up the land line for faxes. The idea behind these choices is that you can call out on your home or fax line (when it's not in use) and leave the business line for incoming calls.

A speaker is also a nice feature, especially for all those on-hold-forever calls to insurance carriers. Your hands are free to enter data, your shoulder remains unhunched, and there's no earring jabbing you in the back of the head while you listen to garbled Muzak® and wait your turn.

You can expect to pay about $100 to $200 for a two-line speakerphone with auto redial, memory dial, flashing lights, mute button, and other assorted goodies.

Automated Answering Service

Since you'll probably be out of the office at least part of every week, picking up billing materials and calling on clients, you'll need a receptionist—and it will probably be automated. If you choose not to go with voice mail from your local phone company, your "secretary" will be an answering machine.

The models on the market now are digital, which, aside from the technical mumbo jumbo, means that they don't have audiotapes to get knotted or broken. There are also all sorts of fancy gizmos complete with caller ID, speakerphones, cordless phones, and 15 kinds of memos, but a good basic model capable of answering your business line can be had for less than $40. For a snazzier cordless phone model that can answer two lines, expect to pay about $150.

> **fun fact** ☺
>
> On the medical timeline, the WHO, developer of the ICD codes, came up with the codes in 1893 as a formalization of the Bertillon Classification or International List of Causes of Death. The acronym ICD is a vestige of the codes' original title.

> **warning**
>
> Remember that coding books are updated annually. Make sure the version you have on hand is the most recent.

Vociferous Voice Mail

Voice mail is the phone company's answer to the answering machine, with a few nice twists. Like an answering machine, voice mail takes your messages when you're not in the office. If you have call waiting, a feature that discreetly beeps to announce an incoming call while you're already on the phone, and you choose not to answer that second call, voice mail will take a message for you. Lots of other fun features, such as your very own voice-mail hell ("If you want information on X, press 2"), are also available in various parts of the country.

Voice-mail costs depend on your local phone company and the features you choose, but you can expect to pay around $10 a month for basic service.

> **tip** (i)
>
> Using Skype or a similar video chat service is an excellent way to connect with clients, especially if it involves conferencing with several people. These services are available for a nominal fee (sometimes free), depending on how you wish to use it. Just remember to comb your hair and change out of your PJs before placing the call.

Rah-Rah Reference Manuals

Your library should contain those runaway bestsellers, *Current Procedural Terminology*, otherwise known as the CPT, and *International Classification of Diseases, Revision 10*, aka ICD-10. You'll also want the hit pick of the medical set, the *HCFA Common Procedure Code System* (HCPCS). If you're going to be filing dental claims, definitely add *Current Dental Terminology*, aka CDT 2016, published by the American Dental Association.

The folks at Optum360 offer great versions of these manuals geared toward individual specialties or as a complete listing, in text versions with punchy graphics on the covers, either online or on CD-ROM. Prices vary depending on what you buy, but as an example, you can download the Encoder Pro package online CD-ROM that contains all the CPT, ICD-9, ICD-10-CM, and HCPCS codes starting at $299.

There are a variety of other sources for coding books out there. For example, Alpha II (formerly Unicor Medical) offers their *Easy Coder* series of ICD-10 books for individual specialties. So, if you are doing billing for, say, a chiropractor, you can score an *Easy Coder* book just for that purpose. These quick-reference specialty books run around $95.

You should also check out Optum360's *Insurance Directory*, which gives addresses and phone and fax numbers for scads of carriers. It also uses fun icons to identify which types of claims the carrier pays (e.g., optical or dental), which carriers accept electronic claims, and which accept HCPCS codes on the commercial claims. You can expect to pay about $80 for this gem.

Form-Fitting

Because of the red ink involved, you'll need to purchase CMS 1500 forms. (The form is only considered "official" when it's the preprinted version done in jazzy red ink.) These forms come imprinted or plain, on plain or continuous-feed paper, two-part or one-part, with sensor (bar code) or without, in boxes of 1,500 to 3,000. You should allocate $35 to $100 per box.

Laugh at Lightning

You should invest in a UPS, or uninterruptible power supply, for your computer system, especially if you live in an area where lightning or power surges are frequent occurrences. If you're a computer newbie, you may not realize that even a flicker of power loss can shut down your computer, causing it to forget all the data you've carefully entered during your current work session or—the ultimate horror—fry your computer's brains entirely. With a

---

► **Read All About It!**

The written word is a powerful learning tool. One of your first steps in your new venture should be to read everything you can, not just about the specifics of medical billing, but about starting a small business and marketing and sales techniques. Blitz the bookstore. Make an assault on your public library. Surf Entrepreneur's online bookstore (https://bookstore.entrepreneur.com/)

Your own business library should contain more than your coding manuals. You'll have the documentation that comes with your software or business opportunity package and your Medicare guides, but you should also check out the following:

- ► *Start Your Own Business, Sixth Edition: The Only Startup Book You'll Ever Need* by The Staff of Entrepreneur Media, Inc. (Entrepreneur Press)
- ► *Guerrilla Marketing in 30 Days* by Al Lautenslager and Jay Conrad Levinson, (Entrepreneur Press)
- ► *Understanding Health Insurance: A Guide to Billing and Reimbursement* by Michelle A. Green, (Delmar Cengage Learning)

Don't stop with these. Immerse yourself in your subject. The more you know, the better MIB you'll be. More suggestions can be found in the Appendix. Read all about it!

UPS in your arsenal, you won't lose power to your system when the house power fails or flickers. Instead, the unit flashes red and sounds a warning, giving you ample time to safely shut down your computer.

Since you'll be working online quite a bit, you want to be sure that your UPS includes phone line protection. You can expect to pay $125 and up for one of these power pals.

> **tip** ⓘ
>
> Bar-coded forms, used to track claims, are required by some carriers and frowned upon by others. Make sure you find out the drill in your area before you order.

Lightning Strikes Again

A surge protector safeguards your electronic equipment from power spikes during storms or outages. Your UPS will double as a surge protector for your computer hard drive, CPU, and monitor, but you will want protection for those other valuable office allies—your printer, fax machine, and copier. They don't need a UPS because no data will be lost if the power goes out, and a surge protector will do the job for a lot less money. If you have a fax machine, be sure the surge protector also defends its phone line. You can expect to pay in the range of $20 to $200.

Cool and Calculating

What do calculators and telephones have in common? A numbered keypad and an important place on your desk. Although your MIB software will do the patient accounting calculations for you, there are always spur of the moment arithmetic questions you can answer more quickly without having to zip around through cyberspace. And with the paper tape, you can check your work. Expect to pay $10 to $25 for a battery-operated model and $30 to $100 for a plug-in job. A full-size adding machine is about $150. Also, don't forget that many smartphones come with calculators, as do computer programs.

> **aha!**
>
> If you plan to generate a lot of paper claims, you might want to look into a postage meter. This is a time saver in the lick-and-stick department, and the standing-in-line-at-the-post-office department, and, with those envelope-sealing gizmos, they can even protect against those pesky paper cuts.

Paper Cloning

The copier is an optional item, probably the least important on the list, but as you grow, you may find it a necessary luxury. Keep in mind that you should never send a piece of paper out of your office unless you've kept a copy. Depending on the size and usage, copiers start around $150 and go up into the thousands of dollars. Plus, you have to keep feeding them toner and the cartridges sell for around $20 to $80 each, depending if you wish to make color copies.

Exemplary Equipment Expenses

To give you an idea of how much you can expect to budget, check out the cost of furniture, equipment, and supplies for two hypothetical medical billing services, Medical Claims Plus and Quality Computerized Claims in Figure 9–2, page 151. Medical Claims Plus, a homebased newbie with no employees except its owner, has monthly gross collections of $900. The fledgling business counts as its equipment resources an inexpensive computer system, an inkjet printer, and the basics in software and reference materials.

Quality Computerized Claims, up and running for three years, make its base in an office in a medical complex, has one full-time employee in addition to the owner, and has monthly gross collections of $12,000. Quality Computerized Claims boasts a top-of-the-line computer system for its owner, an inexpensive computer for its employee, a laser printer, a combo fax machine/scanner, a copier, various reference books, and publishing and marketing software that have caught its owner's eye over the years.

After you have done your shopping, fill in the purchase price next to each item, add up the total, and you'll have a head-start on the "Startup Expenses Worksheet," Figure 6–2 on page 113.

Equipment Expenses

Furniture, Equipment, and Supplies	Medical Claims Plus	Quality Computerized Claims
Computer system (including printer)	$2,000.00	$4,000.00
Fax machine	100.00	700.00
Billing software/business opportunity	700.00	5,000.00
Clearinghouse	300.00	N/A
Other software	350.00	500.00
Phone service	50.00	125.00
Internet service	30.00	70.00
Answering machine	40.00	130.00
Reference manuals	200.00	400.00
Uninterruptible power supply	125.00	250.00
Flash drive or online backup	50.00	80.00
Surge protector	34.00	34.00
Calculator	15.00	50.00
Copier	N/A	700.00
Desk	200.00	600.00
Desk chair	60.00	200.00
Printer stand	N/A	70.00
File cabinet	25.00	200.00
Bookcase	70.00	100.00
Computer/copier paper	25.00	50.00
Blank business cards	15.00	25.00
Letterhead paper	30.00	30.00
Matching envelopes	35.00	35.00
10 x 13 envelopes	14.00	28.00
Legal-sized envelopes	10.00	10.00
Address stamp or stickers	10.00	10.00
Extra printer cartridge	40.00	80.00
Extra fax/toner cartridge	20.00	80.00
Mouse pad	10.00	20.00
Miscellaneous office supplies	100.00	150.00
Total Expenditures	$4,658.00	$13,727.00

FIGURE 9–2: **Equipment Expenses for Two Hypothetical MIB Businesses**

Blowing Your Own Horn

O K, you've passed Medical Insurance 101 with flying colors. You've done your market research, figured out your finances, and persuaded your family to act as in-a-pinch employees. Now you need clients.

As we've often stressed, landing that first client can be the hardest part of the medical billing business. But there are ways to nab that first doctor, and the one after that, and the one after that.

The absolute best way to attract clients is through word-of-mouth. Doctors have a set of jungle drums, a grapevine. Doctors gossip. Like that shampoo commercial where the silken-tressed model tells two friends and "they tell two friends and they tell two friends," doctors also pass the word on. The Napa MIB can attest to this. Once she got her first client, she says, "It rolled from there."

"Yeah," you might be muttering aloud, "but how do I get the first one?"

Relax. You have a lot of options.

People Will Talk

The first option is referrals, or networking, which is really a variation on word-of-mouth. The difference is that with word-of-mouth, you sit back and wait for others to talk about you and send business your way. With networking, you actively seek referrals.

Talk to everybody you know. Let them all in on the exciting news that you're now running a medical billing service. You can start with your own doctor. Next time you see her on a professional basis, tell her about your service. But don't ask directly for her business, as this might put a strain on your relationship.

Chances are, however, that she'll have referrals and probably some tips on how to approach other doctors. Terrific! It's always easier to call other doctors when you can say "Dr. Whatsit suggested I call," or "Dr. Whatsit referred me." People always pay more attention when someone they know has given you the green light.

After you talk to your doctor, call other providers you know directly or indirectly: your children's pediatrician, your husband's internist, your father's cardiologist, your pharmacist and dentist. Using the name of a recognized patient, or being one, can give you a foot in the door.

Once you've tapped out those resources, start approaching physicians who specialize in an area you're interested in. For instance, if you have small children, you might start with pediatricians; if you're into athletics, you could try sports medicine practitioners.

There also are lots of other people you already know who you can put on your networking list. Your attorney, accountant, insurance agent, and real estate agent probably have their own little card files full of physicians and will be happy to make referrals. (After all, you are their client. They want to keep you happy. Besides, most people like helping a fellow businessperson.)

Remember how Kim H. in Virginia went to see her local hospital administrator? He referred her to her first two clients. This is something you can try yourself.

When you're finished with professional types, call your friends. Call your parents. Call your parents' friends. There's nothing parental units like better than helping out some nice young person (no matter what age you feel you are). Can you imagine a motherly type not calling her pal—whose son/cousin/in-law is a doctor—with the news that her best friend Sylvia's daughter is starting a medical billing business and is looking for clients? Of course she will, and you should take advantage of that. Good referrals can come from unlikely sources. And everybody either knows somebody or knows *somebody* who knows somebody. This is what makes networking work.

> **tip** (i)
>
> "I think the biggest fear of people who are getting into this business is how they're going to market themselves," Kim H. offers. "My advice to them is make yourself well-known at first and then when you get that first client, just really work hard and get that money in. Do a really good job, and it's like it just goes from there."

Whatever you do, don't give up! Our Napa MIB said that she didn't get her first client until the almost two-year mark. But once she had her first doctor, the ball immediately started rolling from there because she could use that client as a reference. "I really started growing quickly from that point and never stopped," says Heidi H. "If you keep a good name in this business, they are going to talk about you." Since landing her first client five years ago, her business has expanded to include six employees in two locations. She attributes 65 percent of her success to referrals.

The MIB Letter

Many MIBs have had great success with newsletters or other direct-mail pieces.

"I really think my newsletter did it," the New Jersey MIB says triumphantly. "That got me the two psychologists right off the bat." She also did a few "walk-ins," which netted her another psychologist, who referred her to a psychiatrist.

Along with the newsletter, New Jersey's first mailing included an introductory letter and a sort of resume describing her services.

She now sends out a newsletter to existing clients about every two months, featuring small articles about coding changes—and more. "With mental health, it's good," she says, "because there's so many ways a psychologist who's not bringing in many insurance patients [can increase his income]. He could be making money other ways—by volunteering [his] time at the courthouse, by networking with attorneys."

tip

Online newsletters can further your marketing goals and get your message out to current and prospective customers in a cost-effective, credible manner. Existing and potential clients subscribe to receive articles and informative tips from you, and it puts your business's name in front of them on a regular basis.

This is a good strategy for any potential client newsletter. When you show doctors your expertise in various phases of medical billing or practice management, you give them the confidence to go with your company. You can also make their mouths water. Let them think "Wow, if I had this billing service, I'd have this sort of stuff available all the time."

"I don't gear it just toward billing," the New Jersey biller explains. "I gear it toward other things that they're going to be interested in. I keep them pretty happy with that." Plus, this helps to position yourself as an expert in the medical claims billing industry, which builds credibility. The San Diego MIB landed her first client through a direct-mail survey, which included a cost analysis. But it wasn't a quick sale.

"I worked with the office for about five months before actually signing them," the former nurse says. "I really had to build a good rapport with [the receptionist] because she's the one who answers the phone. I have to go through her to get to the office manager, and I have to go through the office manager before I can get to the doctor. Becoming a friend and ally [with the front office people] is the best thing you can do."

Summer vacations and the likelihood of the office manager going on disability contributed to major holdups in the doctor's decision-making process. "During that time I had to be very patient, very businesslike, and understanding that they weren't just putting me off," the San Diego MIB recalls. "I could have thought 'Oh, you know, they're just putting me off and they don't really want to do this.' And they could have just fallen through the cracks, but I was persistent and stayed with them. And always, before I got off the phone with them, I made a follow-up appointment. So it wasn't like we hung up the phone and I didn't have a guaranteed connection with them again."

Persistence paid off. She landed the doctor and is now doing full-practice management for him.

In her survey, she came up with several questions designed to custom-tailor her sales pitch for each doctor she approached.

aha!

If you have pre-MIB credentials that will reflect positively on your business, such as an RN or a history with an insurance carrier or large billing company, make sure you mention it in your newsletter. Use your history to your advantage!

She asks how much the target office knows about electronic billing so that she can go into the right amount of detail when she makes her in-person pitch. She asks what their claims volume is and what it's costing them to send claims on paper. Another question focuses on which carriers are billed and at what percentage.

"Those are the main things," she says. "And then one of the last things I ask is what their specialty is, how many doctors they have, and how many years they've been in practice."

She averaged a 20 percent return from this mailing, which is a very good response. Look at it this way. If you mail out a similar survey to 100 doctors and net a 20 percent return, that's 20 doctors who have more or less given you an invitation to call on them.

At 'Em Advertising

More traditional forms of advertising such as print ads, TV or radio spots, and Yellow Pages ads don't seem to do as well for the MIB as the methods we've just discussed: calling-all-relatives, networking, and direct mail.

"You have to be really smart about how you invest money for advertising," cautions the Napa MIB. "You could spend thousands and never get the targeted clientele that you want. Medical billing services aren't for the masses, just for the doctor's office." This is a good rule of thumb to focus your marketing efforts on the audience you are trying to reach.

Most of our MIBs are not in favor of using the Yellow Pages, unless it's the online directory, where most people go to look. "If a doctor in your area is looking for a medical billing service, then your name will pop up, so that's a good use of advertising dollars," says the Napa MIB.

If you can get your local Yellow Pages to give you a good rate, an ad couldn't hurt. But you might do better to concentrate your advertising and marketing budget on direct mail. You'll already have a computer. With the desktop publishing programs that are available now, you can afford to experiment. Write up ad copy, and pop in some clip art. Have fun with it.

The San Diego MIB—the one who netted her first client with a survey—has been having a ball with her two desktop publishing programs.

"It's fun," she says. "I'm not a very creative person by nature. It takes a lot of work for me to produce something creatively. When somebody gives me an idea, then I can

tip

Most medical billing services advertise under the heading "Billing." Some advertise under "Insurance" or "Insurance Services" and some under "Medical and Dental Business Administration." Find out what the norm is in your area, then go with one or more of the above.

▶ Direct-Mail Dazzle II

Use the letter in Figure 10–1 on page 159 for your direct-mail ad campaign. You can use it as is by retyping it onto your letterhead, or you can modify it in any manner that feels right to you, but keep in mind the following:

- ▶ Try writing as if you were speaking to a friend. You want your letter to sound professional, of course, but stiff and stodgy doesn't create interest. Keep it peppy!

- ▶ Don't be modest. List by name all industry associations to which you belong and any certifications you have.

- ▶ Don't forget to insert your cost analysis! You can use the survey from Chapter 4 as a template or design your own.

- ▶ Include a SASE (self-addressed stamped envelope), or invite them to your website to fill out an online survey

- ▶ Check to make sure you've spelled the doctor's name and business name correctly!

- ▶ Make sure everything else is spelled correctly and your grammar and punctuation are fine-tuned.

- ▶ Remember to stick to the point. Don't let your words wander.

[say] 'Oh!' It gives me ideas of how to go about it. These templates are great. You just pick the different clip art and then if you want it arranged [differently], then you just change a few things and it's done. I love doing desktop publishing now."

Direct mail is inexpensive compared with some other forms of advertising. When you consider that, aside from your time, your only expenses are stationery and stamps, what have you got to lose? Or to turn it around, what do you have to gain?

aha!

Use your clip art to spark ideas. "In one [mailing] I have," the San Diego biller says, "there's clip art with a little guy with several different hats on, and I'm appealing to the office manager or the doctor, whoever it is that wears many hats in the office."

(Cold) Calling All Clients

If you hated the "ask the fellow" part of Sadie Hawkins dances, or if you were at the bottom of the Cub Scout candy-sales pack because you didn't like knocking on doors, then cold calling (calling on a prospect unannounced) will leave you chilled to the bone.

OLD OAK CLAIMS SERVICES
345 Main Street • Huckleberry, New Hampshire 00001
Phone (000) 000-3456 • Fax (000) 000-3457
www.oldoakclaims.com

June 12, 20xx

Dr. Wally Whatsit
123 North South Street
Huckleberry, NH 00001

Dear Dr. Whatsit:

How would you like to have your patients' bills paid—on time, hassle-free, and without you or your staff having to lift a finger?

My company, Old Oak Claims Services, would like to take insurance claim nightmares and patient billing headaches out of your office, leaving you and your staff free to do what you do best—practice medicine.

My services range from claims filing to full-practice management. I know how to get claims paid quickly and handle billing problems effectively. I don't get paid until you do, so my incentive is strong. I can also provide you with the best in patient accounting, from posting and mailing bills to full accounts receivable operations, including customized reports.

I know I can increase your collections! I'd like to show you how. Simply fill out the enclosed cost analysis and 1) fax it to me at (000) 000-3457, 2) mail it in the enclosed self-addressed stamped envelope, or 3) fill out the online survey at OldOakClaims.com.

I look forward to talking with you and your staff, and tailoring a program for you. Feel free to call me with any questions at (000) 000-3456.

Best regards,

Judy January

Judy January
Old Oak Claims Services

P.S. For a limited time, I am offering a free month of Medicare billing to show you that I'm serious about saving you money!

FIGURE 10–1: **Direct-Mail Piece**

Although general industry reviews are mixed, the MIBs we talked with who have tried this approach were pleased with the results. "What [the business opportunity vendor] said, which I thought made sense," Curt J. says, "is if you don't have any clients yet and you don't have any experience, the only thing you have to sell is yourself. So because I wasn't afraid of face-to-face selling, I just made up my own brochures along with some other material, and I went door to door and gave them my materials. I followed up with another visit and then followed that up with a phone call."

The Montana MIB got her first two clients through cold calling. "I made personal contacts," she says. "I created some quality hand-outs and reply cards, and I do my own personal contacts [by walking] into doctors' offices and leaving information."

The Doctor's World

Calling on doctors is a unique experience. They usually have a chorus line of patients waiting in the wings, colleagues and pharmacists dialing up with questions, and assistants darting back and forth with questions from patients. There's little time for dillydallying, shooting the breeze, or kicking back for a cup of coffee and a chat. If you understand how a doctor's office works, you'll have a better chance of seamlessly insinuating yourself into it.

As with most businesses, the typical health-care office is made up of various personalities, job descriptions, and educational backgrounds. The staff usually includes a receptionist, various office assistants, an office manager and clinical staff help such as nurses, therapists, or hygienists. Let's look at this motley crew to find out who does what:

▶ *Receptionist.* This person's responsibilities vary according to the size of the practice. In a large office, the receptionist may simply answer the phone, but in most practices, she (or he) is also responsible for scheduling appointments, collecting patient information, taking messages, and opening and routing office mail.

▶ *Office assistants.* Large medical and dental practices employ office assistants to help the receptionist with clerical and administrative tasks such as maintaining patient accounts and general bookkeeping. They may or may not have a say in administrative decisions, but it's a smart idea to deal with them as if they do.

▶ *Office manager.* If the physician's practice is large enough to have an office manager, this person is usually responsible for managing the office staff, maintaining patient relations, monitoring accounts and collections, gathering financial information for the doctor and accountant, and overseeing office operations. The doctor usually grants the office manager a great deal of decision-making power. She might have been trained at a trade school and might have several years' experience in health-care administration. Winning over this key staffer can be every bit as important as winning over the doctor. If you succeed in gaining her interest, she should have enough leverage to set up the big meeting between you and her boss, and the doctor will take her suggestions seriously. In some cases, the office manager has the authority to decide on her own whether to use your service.

▶ *Clinical help.* Nurses, therapists, hygienists, and other medical assistants usually work in the back office. They assist the doctor with clinical work and usually have little input when it comes to business decisions.

Handle with Credibility

Because the medical billing industry took off with such a bang, many doctors got burned by MIBs who didn't know the ropes. Business opportunity vendors pulling people off the street put a lot of people in the driver's seat who really didn't belong there. Consequently, a lot of doctors got dinged with heavy fines and even the threat of losing their Medicare billing status. This has, not surprisingly, turned them MIB-shy.

More and more doctors are now receptive to outsourcing, but to some extent they're still skeptical because they've been stung by people who didn't know what they were doing.

This is why most of our MIBs feel that being certified in medical billing and coding is so important. Heidi H. feels it definitely helps if you are certified because doctors are going to come to you with coding problems. "Being certified helps you in about 85 percent of your job," she says. "If you want to land the clients with high volume, you want to be certified to get their attention. You want them to be able to trust you in order to give you their business." Having a certification gives you credibility because it indicates that you have a certain level of knowledge and skill in the industry.

Because the Georgia MIB got an early start in the medical claims billing industry, her knowledge came primarily from on-the-job training—and a lot of trial and error. However, she feels with the recent changes in health-care laws and the inception of ICD-10 codes that certification is a must. "I always recommend the AAPC exams," says Marsha S. "They have different certifications geared toward billing, coding, compliance, and other areas of the medical billing industry."

Sandra S. from Minnesota, recommends taking your education a step further by going to an accredited college and getting your associate's degree in health information management, and becoming certified as a coder and biller. "Taking a transcription course will also help you

tip
Certifications can be obtained by joining professional organizations that offer qualifying educational programs as well as ongoing support services, such as the American Academy of Professional Coders (AAPC).

if you decide to add a transcription side to your business to be a one-stop shop for smaller providers," she advises.

Continuing education on your part is also vitally important. When you point out to potential clients that you really do know your business, that you belong to industry associations and attend classes and seminars on an ongoing basis, your credibility—and your salability—will rise. This indicates to your clients that you are operating within the highest standards of your profession and keeping informed of current trends. In fact, staying current with insurance issues and regulations like HIPAA are key to success in this industry, according to Tammy Harlan, president and CEO of Medical Billing Course, LLC, a medical billing training company in LaPorte, Indiana.

"Training boosts your confidence," says Harlan, who is a former MIB herself. "It also helps you keep up with the changes and complexities of this industry, which makes you more valuable to your clients."

▶ Getting Past the Gatekeeper

In most offices, the doctor is protected from the outside world by a bevy of staffers who have been trained to guard him with their professional lives. These gatekeepers feel it's their job to fend off callers—phone and in-person—so the doctor can do his job uninterrupted.

Getting in to see the doctor without bleeding, sneezing, or limping can sometimes seem an insurmountable task, like breezing in to see the pope on your way through Vatican City.

"For the most part," Curt J. says, "I found three kinds of offices. There were those that, as soon as [the office staff] found out what you were doing, felt threatened or intimidated. A couple commented 'You want my job.' I tried to assure them that's not why I was there." This type of office, he found, represented the minority of those he visited.

The second type was ruled by the office manager. "Getting to them was fairly simple and easy, even if there was a receptionist," Curt says. Of the third category, he says, "Regardless of how big the staff is, the doctor pretty much has his finger in every arena and operation. If that's the case, I was able to get to him fairly easily also."

The Montana biller also found that approaching the doctor was often a cinch. "Many times, the doctors would be there in the area and I would actually visit with them," she says. "It makes it much more personal. They're the ones who are going to make the decision."

It's also a good idea to join a professional organization for referral and networking opportunities. Two that you may want to consider are the American Academy of Professional Coders (AAPC—https://www.aapc.com), and The Professional Association of Healthcare Coding Specialists (PAHCS—www.pahcs.org). Both groups offer educational programs and resources. Being members of professional organizations gives you additional credibility, and you may be allowed to place their logos on your company's printed materials.

Capture That Client

Once you have a doctor sit down and listen to your pitch, how do you close the sale? One way is by sitting on his chest until he yells "OK!" and signs on the dotted line.

This is not recommended. The preferred method is to offer him options he can't refuse. You can offer to bill him on a per-claim basis, hourly, or on a monthly percentage basis.

Percentage Pow!

Let the doctor know that when he pays you a percentage of his collections, you both come out winners. The San Diego MIB pitched her provider this way: "I'd be charging on a percentage of claims, but [your] overhead would come way down."

Obviously, it was a winning pitch because she's now doing full-practice management for him. It worked because she told him he couldn't lose. He'd gain not only in increased collections but also in reduced overhead. He could afford to send his former office manager off on disability because he'd be replacing her with an outsource service for which he did not have to pay hourly wages, workers' compensation insurance fees, or payroll taxes.

The Denver MIB explains her rationale for charging on a percentage basis this way: She says it's her incentive to make sure things are done correctly and that she collects on the claims. "If we don't collect, the doctor doesn't get money, and neither do we."

"I think it would help if providers understood that medical billers have more incentive to push a claim through if they are going to get a percentage vs. nothing," says the Napa MIB. "If they are paying by the claim, then once it's filed the billing service has no incentive to get the claim fixed or paid. I think this is the one thing that makes billing services who charge a percentage stand out."

This is an excellent bargaining table technique. Everyone understands the desire to make money. Put it to the doctor in these same terms; it tells him that you're going to work hard because you want to see cash pile up. When you combine this technique with the facts of lowered overhead and increased collections, you have a hard-to-ignore sales pitch.

The Per-Claim Pitch

You can pitch the per-claim basis by showing the doctor that it costs less to pay you so much per claim than it does to pay an in-house staffer to do the same thing. When you figure in payroll costs and the costs of paper, software, and clearinghouse fees and compare it with your per-claim price, you have a great sales technique.

Use this data as a starting point:

tip ⓘ

Save your hourly basis pitch for offices where the other two methods of pricing just won't work— for example, a provider who sees few patients. Pitch this fee structure the same way you'd pitch per-claim and percentage bases. It's still a good deal for the doctor and still a good deal for you.

- ▶ The cost per claim for a paper claim can reach $18 to $25, compared with just $1 to $3 for an electronic claim, according to the American Medical Association.
- ▶ Less than 1 percent of first-time electronic claims are rejected. They're also paid within 7 to 21 days, vs. 90 to 120 days for paper claims.
- ▶ Doctors can reduce outstanding accounts receivables by more than 60 percent by using electronic claims submission.

Home in on your closing. Point out that your expertise will net the doctor more collected claims. Explain that when you do the claims, that's all you do. Your attention won't be diverted by other demands of a busy office. You're free to concentrate on making sure the claims get paid. His staff is free to take care of patients, and no one needs to worry about follow-up because you'll do it all.

You Must Remember This

Don't undersell yourself. Once you've locked yourself into a contract, you're stuck for the duration. There's nothing like the rocks-in-the-pit-of-the-stomach feeling of signing a client only to discover that that great low, low price you've negotiated won't pay for the time it takes to do the work. Plus, if you've negotiated high enough, when contract renewal time rolls around, you'll meet less resistance with the same fee structure than if you try to bump up your rates.

Don't be discouraged if you don't close the sale on your first meeting. As long as the doctor doesn't bark out a flat "No!" the door is still open. Even if he does say no, you can always go back in a few months and see if things in his office—or in his mind—have changed. Just make sure you set up an opportunity for another phone call or visit before you leave the office.

▶ Forms for Lunch

Along with the contract, work out other details with the doctor and his staff, such as who will handle calls to and from patients regarding their insurance claims and the charges they owe and what you expect the office to provide when you pick up information: superbills, reports, or EOBs you'll need to send with claims, new patient fact sheets, and new insurance information.

You might design a handy checklist for the office to use each time they prepare a folder full of goodies for you or a packet containing materials such as precertification and predetermination forms. All of this is great PR!

Let the doctor help with negotiations. Ask what she needs and wants. Ask what it would take to have her sign with your service.

Curt J. signed his first clients on a per-claim basis, doing electronic filing of claims he entered on his own software. He was very upfront when he started the working relationships. "I told them, 'The reason I am doing this is because I want all your business someday,'" says the former pastor/MIB. "'But I am willing to start doing it this way: a) because you need it, but b) at some point in time you're going to have to upgrade your office. At that point in time, I'm hoping to get all your business.'"

People Who Need People

Here's another excellent technique. Telling the client that you want his business may sound redundant, but it's not. Everybody wants to be wanted (except by the IRS). Everybody wants to feel important. When you bring this into the open, you're telling your prospect that you think enough of him and his business to strive for it. People respond in kind.

A good way to get your potential client to work with you in negotiations is by asking open-ended questions. You want to know the "reporter's six:" what, where, when, why, how, and who. For example, who in the office does the billing currently, how long does it take, when does it get done, etc.? Asking these sorts of questions as opposed to close-ended questions that can be answered with a short "yes" or "no" gets the prospect talking and thinking and gives you the opportunity to respond.

Be creative. If you meet with opposition, think of ways around it. You might, for example, offer a free month's trial service or a waived setup charge. Curt gave a prospective

▶ Putting out a Contract

Once you've convinced the doctor that you can handle his work, it's time to put it in writing in the form of a contract. This is where you establish exactly what each of you will provide the other. Spell out how you will get information from the office (email, snail mail, or delivery), how often you'll send patient statements, what types of reports you'll generate, and at what intervals (once a month, once a quarter).

You'll also need to cover your fee, how often you'll bill the doctor, and when you expect payment. Be sure that you cover termination of the contract, specifying who has the right to terminate it and how much notice they need to give. You should also specify for how long you expect to be paid after you've stopped billing.

You can use the sample "Health-Care Billing Agreement," Figure 10–2 at the end of this chapter on page 172 as is or modify it in any way you choose. After you've fine-tuned it, however, seek a second opinion. "Any agreement," the San Diego biller advises, "should be looked at by an attorney before having a client sign it, to make sure all bases are covered."

client three free months of Medicare filing and then immediately wowed her with claims paid in record time. His strategy is simple but elegant: After three months of such service, she'll be hooked. Not signing a contract to continue his service will seem insane.

When you give free trial service, you're doing three things. One, you're showing the doctor that you have faith in your operations; therefore, they must be good. Two, the learning curve is a freebie, too. If you discover after the trial noncontracted period that you hate the MIB business, you can bow out gracefully. (But of course, you won't.) Three, it lands that first elusive client. After the first one, word-of-mouth and your own increased confidence will carry you along toward more sales.

One Singular Sensation

How you present yourself at a sales presentation is as important as how you present your business. Even if you're doing the actual billing in your blue jeans, you need to show up at your prospective client's office dressed for success. Wear business apparel. Make sure your shoes and briefcase or handbag are clean and/or polished. Check before you leave home to ensure that all sales materials—your business cards, brochures, and any charts or peripheral goodies—are clean, tidy, and organized.

It's a good idea to call ahead to confirm the appointment. Doctors can get tied up with an emergency or a waiting room full of anxious patients. When you arrive, arrive on time. If you're late, you're sending a message that you don't value the doctor's time and that you're not efficient, the exact opposite of the message you want to convey.

It's only natural to be nervous. Don't let it throw you. Doctors are used to people who aren't at their best. They're not expecting you to tap dance into the office with a top hat and cane. (Although that does make a lasting impression.)

Remember that you know what you're talking about. Have faith in yourself, your service, and your abilities. Believe it or not, your confidence will come through. You needn't imagine the doctor stark naked, as professional lecturers sometimes do of their audiences, but do picture him as an equal. He's a professional at his job; you're a professional at yours.

Public Relations Patter

Once you land your first clients, you should continue to promote yourself to them and to new prospects with public relations. The newsletters we've already discussed are excellent PR tools. Through them, you keep your existing clients abreast of new rules and ideas and, with luck, get them to brag about you to their colleagues. When they use the tips you provide, they help you become more efficient. Newsletters also tell your clients that you're still thinking of them even though you already have the contract and that you're always working toward increasing their collections. This helps get your name circulating on the doctor grapevine and also ensures that the doctors you have sign on for another year when renewal comes up.

You can use materials from your newsletters to publish articles in local medical association publications or to give talks for the same associations. You can also pull out promotional material from your brochures.

How about going on the air? Volunteer yourself for a local radio station's chat show. You can use your same materials for discussion. Listeners can call in and ask questions, then tell their doctor they talked to you. If you do a little research to discover which stations doctors and their staff listen to in the office, for instance, you'll get even more of the exposure you want.

tip

Help a Reporter Out (HARO) is a great source for free publicity. Sign up for their daily newsletters at www.helpareporter. com and look through queries from publications across the nation who are looking for experts in different fields. Typically, this can lead to quotes and honorable mentions in articles or reports, and occasionally it can even involve TV and radio interviews.

▶ Alert the Media

Press releases are free publicity spots that expose your business to the community; but to be printed in the news, the information in your release has to be newsworthy. One way this subtle form of self-promotion can be done is by tying the announcement into local community programs, holidays, or national health observances such as American Diabetes Month or Men's Health Week.

Write your press release in the style of a news article. This means it should be informative and factual while avoiding peppy sales jargon and superlatives. Provide interesting information that gets straight to the point by letting readers know how this announcement will benefit them. Although you are essentially advertising your business, you want to avoid this type of slant because self-promotion is not considered newsworthy.

Make up a list of media contacts, including television, radio, newspaper, community organizations, and online sources so that when you are ready, you can plan a press release blitz. Be sure to include your contact information, including your cell phone number and email address. Folks in the media work on tight deadlines, and if they can't reach you right away to ask questions, they may be inclined to drop the story and move on.

If you're aware of a promotional event in town where you think doctors might show up—say, a charity function or golf tournament—offer to help. If the event will aid an environmental cause, you can point out that your services are green—by filing electronically, you use fewer paper products, thus saving trees. The main benefit you'll get from attending these events is that you can meet doctors, shake their hands, and be a familiar face to them. Then, when you call on them, you have a common ground. You can say "Remember me? We met at the Save the Spotted Owl Charity Ball."

Building Your Online Presence

Today, an internet presence is as essential as a telephone and fax machine. A website is your online brochure and it will be working for you 24 hours a day, seven days a week. In addition to credibility, a professional-looking website gives you a variety of marketing opportunities. Heidi H., our MIB from Napa, says that her website has been a good marketing tool for her business because she can direct providers to it to read about her services.

Whether you decide to set up and design your own website or hire someone to do it for you like Heidi did, there are some things you need to think about in advance. Ask yourself the following questions to help with planning your site's structure and design:

▶ Blogging for Business

In addition to having a website, you can also benefit from having a blog, which increases your online exposure to a broad range of potential clients in the medical field by providing articles and tips related to the industry. By regularly posting information on your blog you will automatically improve your search rankings, plus it lets you build brand awareness with visitors. Regular blogging also gives you the opportunity to differentiate yourself from the competition, exploit any niches, manage your own professional reputation, and position yourself as an authority in your field. Connect your blog with social networks like Facebook and Twitter, and you will increase your exposure exponentially.

You can also contact other highly recognized blog owners within your niche or specialty, and offer to write a guest post that will link back to your site.

1. What are the goals of this website? What do you want it to do?
2. Who is the target audience? Know the demographics such as age, gender, location, and socioeconomic information.
3. How will your site benefit your audience? What are you offering people who visit?
4. What is the tone or image for the site? What are the key messages? Are there any themes you want to convey? For example, are there existing pieces the site needs to coordinate with (i.e., printed materials, packaging, signage, logos, etc.)?
5. How do you want visitors to respond to the website? What do you want them to think? Is there something you want them to do? Suggestions would be to sign up for a newsletter or blog.
6. Will the site be promoted? If so, how?

Take Time to Be Sociable

It's true that "time is money," and time spent networking online is critical to the success of promoting your business online. This is a low- or no-cost marketing strategy that can have a global impact while building personal relationships and credibility. Many entrepreneurs have joined this growing trend and are promoting themselves via social networks like Facebook (www.facebook.com), LinkedIn (www.linkedin.com), and Google+ (https://plus. google.com). It's not at all unusual for one entrepreneur to ask another, "Do you twitter?" while referring to the wildly popular micro-blogging service (https://twitter.com) that allows members to send short updates or "tweets" to other users.

Another advantage of social networking sites is that you can build profiles to enhance your visibility and link back to your website. Participating on other popular networking sites such as Pinterest (www.pinterest.com), YouTube (www.youtube.com), and Instagram (www.instagram.com) will provide good search results when others are looking for you, which makes them great resources for maximizing cross promotion for your business.

While it's true that social networking can be time consuming, it can also be very effective when done consistently. Set aside a specific time each day to participate in relevant discussion forums and newsgroups so that you are not easily sidetracked. The biggest investment will be your time, so you don't want to waste it.

Are You Being Served?

Since your clients will be signing a contract, repeat business will not be the problem it can be for a retail company. You still, however, need to be concerned with customer service. An unhappy client will not sign on for another year and will not refer other providers, which, as you know, is where you'll get a great deal of your new business.

The best way to handle your clients is the way the Denver MIB does. "They all feel like they're my only client," she says.

> **aha!**
>
> Host a question-and-answer coffee hour, "Ask the MIB," for doctors' staffers. Once you get them excited, they can pitch the doctor, thus opening the door for you.

Make sure your doctor and his staff feel important, well cared for and in good hands. Return phone calls promptly. Follow up on questions. If you don't know the answer to something, find it. When clients bring a problem to the Illinois MIB that he doesn't readily know how to solve, he doesn't hem and haw. He's honest. He tells his clients, "I'm not really sure; I want to be really exact when I talk to you. Let me find out and get back to you on that."

Kill Them with Kindness

Treat patients the same way you treat the doctor and her staff. Patients will report back to the office on your behavior and your problem-solving abilities. The best way to get an "A" is to make them feel special, too. But sometimes this can be difficult. Patients can be impatient, cantankerous, and cranky, especially when they get a bill they don't understand. How do you respond in such a case?

"Kill them with kindness," the Denver MIB counsels. "It makes them angrier, actually, but at least you feel better when you get off the phone. That's something that I have always,

always drilled into any bookkeepers who have worked for me. You don't give back to them what they're giving to you. That makes no sense, and you just end up in a catfight. There's no production in that.

> **tip** ⓘ
>
> Sign up for Google Alerts (www.google.com/alerts) to find out who is talking about you and your business online. This handy service also helps you keep tabs on a competitor or get the latest news and events on a particular topic.

"If they want to blow off to you, that's fine because you know that it's not [personal]. As long as your information is correct, you know that, yeah, they're angry, they've got a big bill. They're having problems with the insurance company, they can't get it figured out, and you're the person they've called and were able to talk to."

This is the key. To the patients, you're accessible. You're someone to whom they can vent their frustration. Just don't take it to heart.

Always remember that you are your best marketing tool and nothing can beat good old-fashioned customer service. And, good marketing techniques will mean even more when we start crunching the numbers in the next chapter.

Health-Care Billing Agreement

This agreement is made by and between _____ (hereinafter called "Billing Service") located in _____ and _____ (hereinafter called "Provider") located in _____, _____ on this ____ day of _____.

Whereas, Billing Service provides services to health-care providers designed to effectuate the filing of medical insurance claims with governmental authorities and private commercial carriers through electronic and manual means (Claims Processing) and also offers direct billing services to the patient (Billing Services); and

Whereas, Provider desires to engage Billing Service to provide Claims Processing and/or Billing Services as set forth herein.

Therefore, Billing Service and Provider agree as follows:

1. **Billing Service Responsibilities**
   a. *Claims Processing.* Billing Service will pick up claims information from Provider every _____, unless other arrangements have been made and both parties have agreed. Billing Service will file, process, and collect Provider's claims and provide a computer-generated report verifying their receipt by the insurance companies on a _____ basis. The claims will be processed within _____ business days, excluding those that contain errors made by the Provider's office, unless alternate arrangements have been made and both parties have agreed.

   b. *Billing Services.* Billing Service will bill patients for services rendered by Provider on a schedule of _____.

2. **Provider Responsibilities**
   a. *Claims Processing.* Provider agrees to provide certain information regarding patients and their insurance coverage that is necessary to enable Billing Service to file and process medical insurance claims. Billing Service shall not be responsible for any delay in or ability to collect claims due to insufficient information provided by Provider.

   b. *Billing Services.* Provider agrees to submit in a timely manner all necessary billing information to enable Billing Service to bill patients in the time frame required by the Provider.

3. **Provider's Payment of Services**
   a. *Claims Processing.* Provider agrees to pay Billing Service the sum of $_____ per insurance claim filed and processed, or at the rate of _____ percent of the total dollar value of all collections.

   b. *Billing Services.* Provider agrees to pay Billing Service the sum of $_____ per billing prepared and sent to patient, or at the rate of _____ percent of the total dollar value of all patient statements collected.

FIGURE 10–2: **Health-Care Billing Agreement**

Health-Care Billing Agreement

c. Billing Service reserves the right to change the rate of compensation upon submission of thirty (30) days' written notice to Provider.

d. In the event that a claim or billing must be resubmitted due to an error by Billing Service, the same shall be resubmitted at no additional cost to Provider.

e. In the event that a claim or billing must be resubmitted without fault on the part of Billing Service, the same shall be resubmitted by Billing Service and Provider agrees to pay Billing Service the charge set forth herein as if such resubmission were an original submission.

f. Billing Service will provide a month-end invoice with all charges due, with attached monthly reports. Remittance of these charges will be due in full within 10 days. Late payments are subject to a 2 percent late fee, and accounts over 45 days are subject to suspension of services unless prior arrangements have been agreed upon in writing.

4. Designation of Billing Service as Provider's Authorized Agent

Provider hereby appoints and designates Billing Service as its agent for the limited purpose of billing and corresponding with insurers regarding processing and collection of insurance claims, and any insurer or payer of claims is authorized in its dealings with Billing Service as the Agent of Provider for this limited purpose.

5. Relationship of the Parties

Billing Service and its employees and contractors shall at all times be independent contractors and not employees of Provider. Billing Service shall not have any authority to compromise claims or to otherwise bind Provider except as expressly set forth above, and Provider shall have no authority to bind Billing Service.

6. Term of Agreement

a. This Agreement shall be in effect for one (1) year from the date of execution.

b. Either party may terminate this Agreement at any time, with or without cause, by giving thirty (30) days' written notice of termination to the other party. Upon termination of service, Provider agrees to immediately remit to Billing Service all charges and fees owed to date.

7. Confidentiality

a. Billing Service agrees and covenants to keep all information concerning physician and its patients, including personal and financial information, strictly confidential, and Billing Service agrees that it will not disclose any such information to any person or third party except as may be reasonably necessary to file and process claims and/or patient billing.

FIGURE 10–2: **Health–Care Billing Agreement,** continued

Health-Care Billing Agreement

b. Provider agrees and covenants to keep all information concerning Billing Service and its fees strictly confidential; and Provider agrees that it will not disclose any such information to any person or third party except as may be reasonably necessary or with prior consent of Billing Service.

c. The foregoing provisions regarding confidentiality shall survive the termination of the Agreement. Furthermore, the foregoing provisions constitute independent covenants and shall not be discharged by any breach or default of the party seeking their enforcement.

8. Warranty

Billing Service's warranty under this Agreement shall be limited to the rerunning, at its expense, of any inaccurate reports or forms, provided that Provider furnishes verification of the inaccuracy of any such report or form, and provided further that such inaccuracies were caused solely as a result of Billing Service's performance, and provided further that Billing Service shall receive written notice of such inaccuracies within ten (10) days of delivery of the inaccurate materials. Provider agrees that the foregoing constitutes its exclusive available remedy.

9. Limitation of Liability

a. Provider agrees that the foregoing warranty is in lieu of all other warranties, expressed or implied. Provider further agrees to maintain copies of all patient information supplied to Billing Service so that at no time will Billing Service possess data that is not simultaneously maintained in Provider's own office.

b. Billing Service has no liability to Provider if data or records are destroyed by fire, theft, acts of God, or any other cause. In the event of system malfunction, for whatever reason, or inability to access the computer, Billing Service shall not be liable for damage to or loss of any Provider data that has been entered into the computer system. However, Billing Service will use its best efforts to minimize the possibility of such damage to or loss of Provider data by use of regular backup procedures.

c. Provider agrees to hold Billing Service harmless from liability resulting from violations of state or federal laws or regulations relating to the extension of credit or handling of accounts receivable by Provider. Provider agrees to aid in the defense of Billing Service in any such state or federal proceeding.

The parties hereto have executed this Agreement as of the day and year set forth above.

Provider

By: _____

Billing Service

By: _____

FIGURE 10–2: **Health-Care Billing Agreement,** continued

Controlling Your Finances

W hether you are a chronic number cruncher or one of the finance-phobic, you'll want to give your company periodic financial check-ups. "Why?" you ask. "I already did all that math stuff in the startup chapter." That was the prenatal exam for the precious baby that's your business. When you've gone through the birthing process and that precocious tot is toddling around, you'll want well-child checkups to make sure your business is as healthy as you imagine.

If there is a problem, you will find out before it becomes critical. For example, if you discover that your per-claim charge barely covers your expenses, you can quickly change gears and raise your price or fee basis before signing another client at the same too-low rate. You can also take measures such as switching to a less expensive clearinghouse, cutting back on mailings, or axing those gorgeous but expensive six-color brochures from the printer in favor of those banged out on your own printer.

Financial checkups don't have to be negative. They can give you a rosy glow by demonstrating how well you are doing—possibly even better than you expected. If you have been saving for a new printer or software program, or if you are hoping to take on an employee, you can judge how close you are to achieving that goal.

Tracking your percentage of collected claims will also give your success rate. If it's high, you can use it to convince new providers to come on in—the water's fine. If it's lower than you thought, now's the time to re-evaluate your billing techniques and make the necessary changes.

Making a Statement

An *income statement* (also called a *profit and loss statement*) charts the collections and operating costs of your business over a specific period of time, usually a month. Check out the income statements in Figures 11–1 on page 177 and 11–2 on page 178 made for two hypothetical medical billing services, Acme and Zephyr. Acme is a newbie, just starting out with one client, while Zephyr, which has been up and running for two years, is breezing along with four clients. Although Acme bills per claim and Zephyr takes a percentage of fees collected, they both cast their income statements the same way.

Acme processes 300 claims per month and charges $3 per claim. Zephyr collects an average of $40,000 per client each month from which a 7 percent commission is deducted. Acme, a one-woman band, is owner-operated and has its home base in the guest bedroom. Zephyr has one full-time employee and makes its base in a downtown office. Neither owner draws a salary; they both rely on a percentage of the net profit for their income.

You will notice that several expense categories have been left blank. We have listed them so you can get an idea of what you might want to use in your income statement. Feel free to tailor your statement to your particular business. If you don't have these categories, leave them out. Use the worksheet in Figure 11–3, page 179, to chart your own income statement. You'll be surprised how much fun finances can be!

To make your statement really right, you need to prorate items that are paid annually, such as business licenses, tax-time accounting fees, or clearinghouse annual fees, and

Acme Medical Billing Service Income Statement
for the Month of June 20XX

Income		
	Monthly collections	$900.00
	Gross monthly profit	$900.00
Expenses		
	Clearinghouse fees	$120.00
	Rent	
	Phone/utilities	25.00
	Postage/delivery	10.00
	Licenses/taxes	
	Employees	
	Benefits/taxes	
	Ad/promo	100.00
	Legal services	
	Accounting services	
	Office supplies	20.00
	Maintenance	
	Transportation	15.00
	Insurance	
	Subscriptions/dues	8.00
	Miscellaneous	50.00
Total Monthly Expenses		**$348.00**
Net Monthly Profit		**$552.00**

FIGURE 11–1: **Income Statement for Acme Medical Billing Service**

Zephyr Medical Billing Service
Income Statement for the Month of June 20XX

Income		
	Monthly collections	$11,200.00
	Gross monthly profit	$11,200.00
Expenses		
	Clearinghouse fees	$480.00
	Rent	500.00
	Phone/utilities	400.00
	Postage/delivery	300.00
	Licenses/taxes	
	Employees	1,750.00
	Benefits/taxes	350.00
	Ad/promo	500.00
	Legal services	
	Accounting services	
	Office supplies	40.00
	Maintenance	
	Transportation	25.00
	Insurance	90.00
	Subscriptions/dues	8.00
	Miscellaneous	50.00
Total Monthly Expenses		**$4,493.00**
Net Monthly Profit		**$6,707.00**

FIGURE 11–2: **Income Statement for Zephyr Medical Billing Service**

Income Statement Worksheet

For the month of _____

Income		
	Monthly collections	$
	Gross monthly profit	$
Expenses		
	Clearinghouse fees	$
	Rent	
	Phone/utilities	
	Postage/delivery	
	Licenses/taxes	
	Employees	
	Benefits/taxes	
	Ad/promo	
	Legal services	
	Accounting services	
	Office supplies	
	Maintenance	
	Transportation	
	Insurance	
	Subscriptions/dues	
	Miscellaneous	
Total Monthly Expenses		$
Net Monthly Profit		$

FIGURE 11–3: **Income Statement Worksheet**

pop those figures into your monthly statement. For example, if you pay a clearinghouse annual "membership" fee of $300, divide this figure by 12 and add the resulting $25 to your clearinghouse expense. This will bump up your monthly clearinghouse expense of, say, $120, to $145, but it will also give you an accurate picture of what your costs are throughout the year.

Dud Doctors

You may encounter a situation in which you have plenty of clients to net a profit, your collections are humming along, and yet your income is low. You've run into the Case of the Dud Doctor, the one who can't seem to pay his account with you. This is not a frequent problem in the medical billing world, but it does happen.

Kim H. faced this difficulty with one of her first clients. "The money he was getting in he was spending rather than paying his bills," she explains. The root of the problem went beyond the doctor himself. "When I went through my training, they said you have to watch physicians' wives and see how closely they're involved in the business. That's a real true statement, because the wife got involved and felt that the claims weren't coming in fast enough, so they wouldn't pay me." In essence, the claims were coming in rapidly, but the doctor and his wife used slow reimbursement as an excuse for not coughing up the fees.

Kim handled the situation in a professional manner, deftly lobbing the problem into the doctor's court. "We talked about it," she explains. "At first I went and said, 'I really don't think it's a good idea; maybe we should terminate our contract,' and that I would stay with him [until] he could find somebody else, but things worked out. He's paying me, and his money's coming in, and he's getting his financial situation straightened out.

"That was a biggie," she adds with some relief. "That was probably [the] only major problem that I've ever had."

The Walnut Creek biller, with ten years of experience and more than 50 physicians to her credit, encounters few payment problems. "They are all very honorable people," she says of her clients. Of her creed, "Pay the bill in a timely manner or we stop doing [your] work," she adds, "I've had people test me a little bit to find out if I really will, and when they find out I really do, then they're fine."

tip

Send your monthly invoice along with your monthly report of how much you've billed—and collected—for your provider. The invoice won't hurt him as much when he can immediately compare it with the report. Plus, it gets your bill noticed quickly!

For more payment collection tips as well as other good information, check out Entrepreneur's *Start Your Own Business, Sixth Edition.*

The Tax Man Cometh

Just as into each life a little rain must fall, so from each business a little tax must be paid. If your budget allows, you should also engage an accountant. You probably won't need her for your daily or monthly concerns, but it's well worth the expense to have someone in the know holding the reins when it comes to April 15, or for those rare Panicsville questions that come up now and again.

tip ⓘ

You can call the IRS with questions at convenient 800 numbers all over the country. You might have to go through Voice-Mail Hell and a lengthy hold period, but once you get a live being on the line, he or she will be surprisingly friendly.

Your tax deductions should be about the same as those for any other small or homebased business. You can deduct a percentage of your home office so long as you're using it solely as an office. These deductions include all normal office expenses plus interest, taxes, insurance, and depreciation (this is where the accountant comes in handy). The IRS has added in all sorts of permutations, for example, that the total amount of the deduction is limited by the gross income you derive from the business activity minus all of your other business expenses apart from those related to the home office. And you thought that new board game you got for Christmas had complicated rules!

Basically, the IRS doesn't want you to come up with so many home office deductions that you end up paying no taxes at all. If, after reading all the lowdown, you're still confused, consult your accountant.

What else can you deduct?

▶ *Business-related phone calls*
▶ *The cost of business equipment and supplies* (again, so long as you're truly using them solely for your business)
▶ *Subscriptions to professional and trade journals*
▶ *Auto expenses.* These accrue when you drive your trusty vehicle in the course of doing business or seeking business. In other words, you're chalking up deductible mileage when you motor out to your clients' offices to pick up superbills or day sheets, or when you take a spin to Dr. Whosit's office to make a sales presentation.
   It's wise to keep a log of your business miles. You can download a handy-dandy app on your smartphone or tablet, or buy a mileage log at your local office-supply store. You can even make one yourself. Keep track as you go. It's no fun to have to

backtrack at tax time and guesstimate how many miles you drove to how many clients how many times during the year.

▶ *Entertainment expenses.* Think wining and dining Dr. Whatsit during the course of a sales pitch or hosting Dr. Whosit's staff at a coffee hour. Keep a log of all these expenses as well, especially if they come to less than $75 a pop (you don't technically need to keep receipts for these), and if you're entertaining at home, have your clients or prospects sign a guest book.

warning

Although the IRS allows attendance at conventions, they've apparently watched too many documentaries about luxury liners. They draw the line at conventions held on cruise ships.

You must have a business-related purpose for entertaining, such as a sales presentation or a Q&A session. General goodwill toward your fellow medical professionals doesn't cut it, so be sure your log contains the reason for the partying.

▶ *Travel for business purposes.* If you attend a seminar or train with your business opportunity vendor, you can deduct air fares, bus tickets, rental car mileage, and the like.

▶ *Hotels and meals.* Since the IRS allows deductions for any such trip you take to expand your awareness and expertise in your field of business, it makes sense to take advantage of any conferences or seminars that you can attend.

Paper or Plastic?

Most small-business owners find it helps if they are able to accept credit and debit cards. That's because many of today's consumers prefer to pay with plastic, whether for convenience, security, reward points, or out of habit.

Fortunately, it's much easier to get merchant status than it has been in the past; in fact, these days merchant status providers are competing aggressively for your business. To get a credit card merchant account, start with your own bank. There are several options available that include accepting online payments or using your laptop, smartphone, or tablet for "mobile checkout." Another easy alternative is using a third-party processor such as PayPal (www.paypal.com).

tip

The IRS loves documentation. The more receipts and logs you accumulate and carefully organize, the happier you'll be if the "A" word (audit) rears its ugly head. The more documentation the better. The IRS can disallow anything without it.

Many of your clients will prefer to write you a check, so look for several key items when accepting them. Check the date for accuracy. Do not accept a check that is undated, postdated, or more than 30 days old. Be sure the written amount and numerical amount agree, or the bank will kick the check back and delay clearance.

On your contract, include a statement describing the methods of payment (cash, specific credit cards, checks) you accept. That way clients won't be surprised when they try to pay with a method you do not accept.

Operating Successfully (or Pulling the Plug)

Most people succeed in the medical billing field by following the tried-and-true business methods of persistence and plain old-fashioned hard work, with a healthy dose of optimism liberally sprinkled throughout. If we've illustrated anything in this book, we hope it's that becoming an MIB involves a lot of work. It's rewarding and sometimes exhilarating work, but it's darn hard work nonetheless.

We also hope we've managed to convey that becoming an MIB is not the same as becoming an overnight success. It takes a lot of knocking on doors to achieve that first client and more knocking to land the ones that follow.

Ground Zero

When the MIBs interviewed for this book were asked what they would do differently if they could start over from ground zero, they gave—not surprisingly—some very honest responses.

tip

Keep your company growth factor at a comfortable level. "I'm not out for quantity," says the biller in Denver. "I'm out for quality. I'm only taking on accounts when I know that the ones I now have are running smoothly. I'm not for [just] numbers because then you start losing."

"I would plan for more hours," the Illinois MIB says. "The marketing end was definitely more time-consuming than I originally scheduled."

Time was also a concern for the Montana biller, who was holding down a full-time job as a bookkeeper while she was landing and then billing for her first clients. "I felt I couldn't put as much into it as I would have liked in the beginning," she says. She also admits, however, that being able to work at outside employment while starting a new business is an advantage—you still have to buy groceries. Wearing two hats was the hardest part, but she's quick to add, "I'm still glad that I've done it the way I've done it."

"I would be more careful about how fast I grew," the Denver biller says. "At one point I grew too fast, and I started to feel like I was losing control of things, and [the clients] couldn't get the personalized service. So I would be very careful about growth and make sure that I did not shortchange any of my physicians."

The teacher, Kim H. in Virginia, attributes much of her success to having chosen the right business opportunity vendor, one she feels comfortable with and one who offers a lot of support. "I'm being honest about this," she says. "Things have gone really good and really smooth."

Get Connected

Heidi H., the MIB from Napa, California, told us that there are dozens of professional medical claims billing forums on Facebook. "I recommend anyone starting an MIB service getting on one of these billing forums," she advises. "You can watch people's questions and answers, and learn a ton of things. The forums are very educational and informative, and act like a mentor in themselves because you have so many knowledgeable MIBs on there from all walks of life and all different specialties."

Many of the medical billing organizations and associations (some are listed in the Appendix) also have member forums that MIBs can participate on and ask questions. You may even be able to "pay it forward" by providing answers to other members.

Problem Children

When asked, three of the MIBs quickly identified the "problem children" that made them lose sleep or slam the phone down. The Napa MIB, who has already confessed to being a phone slammer (not to be confused with the illegal practice of switching phone service), says that her problem kids are the HMOs, especially the Medicare HMOs. "A lot of times the doctors don't get authorization to see the patient beforehand and we'll get a lot of denied claims," she says.

Sandra S., the Minnesota MIB, said that she found the out-of-network providers are the hardest to work with. "Their claims are paid at a lower rate, they do not want to take any reduction in fees, and are just harder to process claims for."

The exchange insurance plans and Blue Cross Blue Shield were the ones who made the Georgia MIB, Marsha S., scratch her head. "BCBS is always a problem child," she says. She also told us to add out-of-network plans to the problem child list. "They pay on UCR rates, but they refuse to disclose what the UCR rates are, so there is NO way possible to estimate what the patient will owe. That makes patients angry."

The Best Reward

Needless to say, being a medical claims biller and coder can be demanding. And, it can also be very rewarding. Sandra S., the Minnesota MIB, loves doing research, digging around for answers, and then seeing the project through to completion. "Doing a good job is truly its own reward for me," she says. She advises future MIBs to become certified, get real-world experience, and remember to have a sense of humor. "We deal with very personal issues and sometimes it is really easy to become overwhelmed."

The Georgia MIB enjoys seeing the positive impact she makes on the bottom line for a practice because it means she's helping the livelihood of practice employees. But perhaps the best part is being able to help the patients, especially those who are already overwhelmed with long-term illness, cancer, or other scary medical problems navigate the tricky waters of medical bills. "I think one great way to use our expertise as MIBs is to actually help the patients we work with get the full benefit out of the insurance policy for which they have paid," Marsha S. says. "It benefits us as well, financially of course, but also in terms of patient satisfaction, which can also turn into more business."

The Quality of Life

At some point during your business's first year of life, you will want to run a happiness checklist. Are you operating successfully? Is your quality of life fulfilling? Or should you pull the plug?

Whether or not you're earning money, the success of your business is contingent on a happiness factor. Because it is a lot of work and a lot of responsibility, you might discover that you'd be just as happy—or even more so—working for someone else. With everything you will have learned, you'll be a great job candidate.

None of the people interviewed for this book seem to have any intention of packing it in. The Montana MIB seemed to mirror the thoughts of all when she said she's excited about having her own business despite the hard work. "You're putting into it as much as you can to be able to have the advantages later on," she says.

> **aha!**
>
> Start a local MIB support group. The San Diego MIB found kindred souls in her area on the internet and through referrals from her business opportunity. These fellow MIBs have become friends and mentors. She plans to meld them into a group that meets once a month or more to discuss common goals and problems.

She also doesn't let cold calling faze her. Rather, she gives it the Schwab's Drug Store approach, like a movie star on the verge of discovery. "It's surprising how you have to be at the right place at the right time," she says, "but that's all it takes."

Likewise, the biller in San Diego refuses to be bothered by the competition. There is some competition in her area, she says, but there are more than enough doctors. "Every billing center can't be everywhere; there's plenty of business to be had," she contends.

These seem to be the attitudes of all the MIBs who so generously helped with this book. Winning attitudes. If you go into the business with the right stuff—a willingness to work hard and to learn everything you can; the confidence to promote yourself and your business; and the drive to succeed—chances are you will.

Medical Claims Billing Resources

They say you can never be rich enough or young enough. While these could be argued, we believe "You can never have enough resources." Therefore, we present for your consideration a wealth of sources for you to check into, check out, and harness for your own personal information blitz.

These sources are tidbits, ideas to get you started on your research. They are by no means the only sources out there and they should not be taken as the Ultimate Answer. We have done our research, but businesses—like patients—do tend to move, change, fold, and expand. As we have repeatedly stressed, do your homework. Get out and start investigating.

As an additional tidbit to get you going, we strongly suggest the following: If you haven't yet joined the internet age, do it! Surfing the internet is like waltzing through a vast library, with a breathtaking array of resources literally at your fingertips.

Associations

American Association of Healthcare Administrative Management, 11240 Waples Mill Road, #200, Fairfax, VA 22030, (703) 281-4043, fax (703) 359-7562, www.aaham.org

American Business Women's Association, 11050 Roe Ave., Ste. 200, Overland Park, KS 66211, (800) 228-0007, www.abwa.org

American Dental Association, 211 E. Chicago Ave., Chicago, IL 60611, (312) 440-2500, www.ada.org

American Marketing Association (AMA), 311 S. Wacker Drive, Suite 5800, Chicago, IL 60606, (800) AMA-1150 or (312) 542-9000, Fax: (312) 542-9001, www.ama.org

American Medical Association, AMA Plaza, 330 North Wabash Ave., Suite 39300, Chicago, IL 60611-5885, (800) 262-3211, www.ama-assn.org/ama

Direct Marketing Association, 1333 Broadway, Suite #301, New York, NY 10018, (212) 768-7277, Fax: (212) 302-6714, http://thedma.org/

Healthcare Billing and Management Association, 2025 M Street NW, Suite 800, Washington, DC 20036, (877) 640-HBMA (4262), fax (202) 367-2177, www.hbma.org

Medical Association of Billers, 2620 Regatta Dr., Suite 102, Las Vegas, NV 89128, http://physicianswebsites.com/

National Health Care Anti-Fraud Association, 1220 L Street, NW, Suite 600, Washington, DC 20005, (202) 659-5955, fax (202) 785-6764, www.nhcaa.org

(*Note*: Just about every medical specialty has a professional organization, which you can find by calling a specializing physician or by checking the internet.)

Books

Start Your Own Business, Sixth Edition: The Only Startup Book You'll Ever Need, The Staff of Entrepreneur Media, Inc., (Entrepreneur Press)

The Best of Guerrilla Marketing—Guerrilla Marketing Remix, Jay Conrad Levinson and Jeannie Levinson, (Entrepreneur Press)

Understanding Health Insurance: A Guide to Billing and Reimbursement, Michelle A. Green and Jo Ann C. Rowell, (Delmar Cengage Learning)

The Ultimate Small Business Advisor—comes with spreadsheet CD-ROM), Andi Axman, (Entrepreneur Press)

Ultimate Guide to Local Business Marketing, Perry Marshall and Talor Zamir, (Entrepreneur Press)

The Marketing Plan Handbook: Develop Big-Picture Marketing Plans for Pennies on the Dollar Paperback, Robert W. Bly, (Entrepreneur Press)

Write Your Business Plan: Get Your Plan in Place and Your Business off the Ground, The Staff of Entrepreneur Media, Inc., (Entrepreneur Press)

Certification and Education

American Academy of Professional Coders (AAPC), 2233 S Presidents Dr., Suite F, Salt Lake City, UT 84120, 800-626-2633, https://www.aapc.com

American Medical Billing Association (AMBA), 2465 E. Main, Davis, OK 73030, (580) 369-2700, fax: (580) 369-2703, www.ambanet.net/AMBA.htm

The Board of Medical Specialty Coding and Compliance (BMSC), Two Washingtonian Center, 9737 Washingtonian Blvd., Suite 200, Gaithersburg, MD 20878,(800) 897-4509, www.medicalspecialtycoding.com

Medical Association of Billers, 2620 Regatta Dr., Suite 102, Las Vegas, NV 89128, http://physicianswebsites.com/

NAHAEC, LLC (National Academy for Healthcare Administration Education and Certification), Medical Billing Course, 3101 Browns Mill Rd., Suite 6103, Johnson City, TN 37604, (888) 274-2745, www.medicalbillingcourse.com

Practice Managers Resource and Networking Community, www.billerswebsite.com

The Professional Association of Healthcare Coding Specialists (PAHCS), 218 E. Bearss Ave. #354, Tampa, FL 33613, (800) 626-2633, www.pahcs.org

Healthcare Resources

AIS Compliance, Atlantic Information Services, Inc. (a company that provides specialized business information for health-care managers), 1100 17th St. NW, #300, Washington, DC 20036, (800) 521-4323, fax (202) 331-9542, http://aishealth.com

American Hospital Association, 155 N. Wacker Drive, Chicago, IL 60606, (800) 424-4301, www.aha.org

Blue Cross and Blue Shield Association, 225 N. Michigan Ave., Chicago, IL 60601, (888) 630-2583, www.bcbs.com

Centers for Medicare and Medicaid Services, 7500 Security Blvd., Baltimore, MD 21244, (800) 633-4227, www.cms.gov

Novitas Solutions (formerly Highmark Medicare Services), 2020 Technology Parkway, Suite 100, Mechanicsburg, PA 17050, (877) 235-8073, www.novitas-solutions.com (Although this site is for providers who handle Medicare for DC, DE, MD, NJ, and PA, their website contains lots of information of interest and value to anybody in the health insurance industry.)

General Small Business Resources

BizFilings, information on incorporating and related services for business owners, including forms, advice, and tools needed, 8025 Excelsior Drive, Suite 200, Madison, WI 53717, (800) 981-7183, (608) 827-5300, www.bizfilings.com

BPlans.com, free sample business plans, articles, and online tools, 44 West Broadway, Suite 500, Eugene, OR 97401, (800) 229-7526, fax: (888) 498-6132, www.bplans.com

Business Finance, thousands of business loan and capital sources, 909 N Sepulveda Blvd. 11th FL, El Segundo, CA 90245, (800) 835-8857, www.businessfinance.com

BusinessUSA, business tools and resources on how to start and finance a new business, and learn about the latest regulations, http://business.usa.gov/

Center for Business Planning, sample business plans and planning guidelines for business owners, Georgetown, TX 78628, (800) 423-1228, http://businessplans.org/

Find Law for Small Business, links to regulatory agencies, sample forms and contracts, articles on all aspects of business development, 610 Opperman Drive, Eagan, MN 55123, (800) 455-4565, fax (800) 392-6206, http://smallbusiness.findlaw.com

The Small Business Advisor, lots of articles and advice for startup businesses, Box 579, Great Falls, VA 22066, (703) 450 7049, fax: (925) 226 4865, www.isquare.com

Website Marketing Plan, 9051 Watson Road, Suite 318, St. Louis, MO 63126, www.websitemarketingplan.com

Government Resources

Affordable Care Act (ACA), U.S. Department of Health & Human Services, 200 Independence Avenue, S.W., Washington, D.C. 20201, (800) 368-1019, www.hhs.gov/healthcare

Centers for Medicare & Medicaid Services, 7500 Security Boulevard, Baltimore, MD 21244, www.cms.gov

HealthCare.gov (managed by the U.S. Department of Health & Human Services), 465 Industrial Blvd, London, KY 40750-0001, (800) 318-2596, www.healthcare.gov

Health Insurance Portability and Accountability Act (HIPAA), U.S. Department of Health & Human Services, 200 Independence Avenue, S.W., Washington, DC 20201, (800) 368-1019, www.hhs.gov/hipaa/

Internal Revenue Service, 1111 Constitution Ave. NW, Washington, DC 20224, (800) 829-4933, www.irs.gov

InsureKidsNow (provides information about Children's Health Insurance Program (CHIP), and Medicaid), 877-543-7669, www.insurekidsnow.gov

Medicare Handbook, U.S. Government Printing Office, 732 N. Capitol Street NW, Washington, DC 20401, (866) 512-1800, (202) 512-1800 (DC area), http://bookstore.gpo.gov

Small Business Administration, 409 Third St. SW, Washington, DC 20416, (800) 827-5722, www.sba.gov

TRICARE (Government health care program serving Uniformed Service members, retirees and their families worldwide), www.tricare.mil

U.S. Department of Health and Human Services, 200 Independence Ave. SW, Washington, DC 20201, (877) 696-6775, www.hhs.gov

Internet Resources

Dropbox, online backup service, www.dropbox.com

FaceTime, video chat service, www.apple.com/mac/facetime

GoDaddy, full service web solutions: domains, web hosting, site building, and SSL certificates, www.godaddy.com

Google Hangouts, video conferencing, https://hangouts.google.com

Mozy, online backup service, http://mozy.com

Register.com, web hosting, domain name, e-commerce, email, e-marketing services, and technology solutions, www.register.com

RingCentral, cloud-based communications system, www.ringcentral.com

Skype, video chat service, www.skype.com

Vistaprint, online printing service, www.vistaprint.com

Vonage, cloud-based communications system, www.vonage.com

Yahoo Groups (online discussion forums), http://groups.yahoo.com

Medical Claims Software, Clearinghouses, and Business Opportunities

American Business Systems, LLC, 5751 Kroger Dr. Ste. 113, Keller, TX 76244, (866) 565-8413, www.absystems.com

ClaimTek Systems, 3943 Irvine Blvd. #39, Irvine, CA 92602-2400, (800) 224-7450, www.claimtek.com/

CollaborateMD, 225 East Robinson St., Suite 145, Orlando, FL 32801, (877) 480-6517, www.collaboratemd.com

MediPro, 1301 Shiloh Road, Suite 1250, Kennesaw, GA 30144, (855) 433-5240, www.medipro.com

Nextech Systems, 5550 West Executive Drive, Suite 350, Tampa, FL 33609, (813) 425-9200, www.nextech.com

Office Ally, PO Box 872020, Vancouver, WA 98687, (360) 975-7000, https://cms.officeally.com

ZirMed, 888 West Market Street, Louisville, KY 40202, 855) 933-1345, http://public.zirmed.com/

Online Postage

Pitney Bowes, Inc., 2225 American Drive, Neenah, WI 54956, (800) 243-7824Fax: (800) 882-2499, www.pitneybowes.com

Stamps.com, 1990 E. Grand Ave, El Segundo, CA 90245-5013, (855) 889-7867, www.stamps.com

United States Postal Service (USPS), (800) 275-8777, www.usps.com

Professional Journals and Newsletters

BC Advantage magazine, PO Box 80669, Simpsonville, South Carolina 29680, (877) 700-3002, www.billing-coding.com/

The Coding Institute (newsletters for coding, billing, compliance and reimbursement guidance), 2222 Sedwick Road, Durham, NC 27713, 800-508-2582, www.codinginstitute.com

Healthcare Business Monthly (from AAPC), 2233 S Presidents Dr., Suite F, Salt Lake City, UT 84120, 800-626-2633, www.aapc.com

Medical Economics® magazine, (owned by Avanstar Communications), One Park Ave., New York, NY 10016, (212) 951-6600, fax (212) 951-6793, http://medicaleconomics. modernmedicine.com

The Profitable Practice (Software Advice), 200 Academy Drive, Suite 120, Austin, Texas 78704, (800) 918-2764, http://profitable-practice.softwareadvice.com

Reference Books

American Medical Association, Publications, AMA Plaza, 330 N. Wabash Ave., Chicago, IL 60611-5885 (800) 621-8335, www.ama-assn.org

CDT: Code on Dental Procedures and Nomenclature, American Dental Association, 211 East Chicago Ave., Chicago, IL 60611-2678, (312) 440-2500, http://www.ada.org/en/publications/cdt

Optum360, Coding and Reference Materials, 2525 Lake Park Blvd., Salt Lake City, UT 84120, (800) 464-3649, www.optum360coding.com/

http://MD Code Wizard, www.mdcodewizard.com/

Medical Terminology Dictionary

> ▶ MediLexicon: www.medilexicon.com/medicaldictionary.php
> ▶ GlobalRPh: www.globalrph.com/medterm.htm

PMIC (Practice Management Information Corp.), Coding and Compliance Solutions, 4727 Wilshire Blvd., #300, Los Angeles, CA 90010, (800) MED-SHOP, fax (800) 633-6556, http://pmiconline.stores.yahoo.net/

Seminars

McVey Associates, Inc., 150 Ford Way, Suite 100, Novato, CA 94945, (800) 227-7888, www.mcveyseminars.com

Southern Medical Association, 35 W. Lakeshore Drive, Birmingham, AL 35209, (800) 423-4992, http://sma.org

(*Note*: Check with the professional organizations for the specialties you'll be billing to see if they schedule seminars.)

Successful Medical Billing Services

Account Resolutions, LLC, Mary J. Vandegrift, 8775-P Cloudleap Ct., PMB 46, Columbia, MD 21045, (443) 259-0660, email: maryvande@aol.com

Medical Billing Systems of Rockford, Curt Johnson, P.O. Box 4782, Rockford, IL 61110, (815) 226-0669

Sandra Shepard, Waconia, MN, http://bit.ly/Upwork-Shepard

Marsha Sosebee, CHCS, 908 N. Dick Creek Rd. Lafayette, GA 30728, marshasosebeechcs@gmail.com

Valley Medical Billing Services, Heidi Horning, P.O. Box 4061, Napa, CA 94558, 800-807-9843, www.valleybillingservices.com

Glossary

Accept assignment: term meaning the provider accepts Medicare's approved fee for his services

Administrative Services Only (ASO): *see* Third-party administrator

Administrator: the insurance company that writes and administers the insurance policy; also known as the insurer, underwriter, or carrier

Affordable Care Act (ACA): health reform legislation signed into law in March 2010; also referred to as Obamacare

Allowable: the portion, usually 70 to 80 percent, paid by the insurer for covered services

Annual maximum: maximum amount a policy will pay in a benefit year or calendar year, depending on the terms of the policy for elective or non-essential health benefits

Antigen: substance that induces the formation of antibodies

Audit/error report: report generated by the clearinghouse to notify biller of rejected claims; also called a sender log

Basic plan: commercial plan that pays total costs up to a stated maximum for all but a few exclusions; costs may be incurred in the hospital, at the doctor's office, or at home; may or may not feature deductible

Beneficiary: the person eligible to receive benefits under the insurance policy; the patient

Benefits verification: *see* Predetermination

Birthday rule: in cases of multiple dependent insurance coverage, the determination of primary coverage by parents' birth dates

Carrier: the insurance company that writes and administers the insurance policy; also known as the insurer, underwriter, or administrator

CDT: common name for dental terminology; system of coding dental and orthodontic procedures, updated on an annual basis

Centers for Medicare and Medicaid Services (CMS): previously known as the Health Care Financing Administration (HCFA)

Certificate holder: *see* Insured

Certification: the act of attesting that an individual or organization has met a specific set of standards

Charge slip: *see* Superbill

Civilian Health and Medical Program for the Uniformed Services (CHAMPUS): provides dependents of active and retired military personnel and their families with civilian health-care coverage

Claims processing: the process of receiving, investigating, adjusting,c and remitting an insurance claim

Clean claim: one that does not need correction

Clearinghouse: a company that receives and transmits claims electronically

CMS 1500: form on which all medical insurance claims must be sent, formerly known as the HCFA 1500

Code modifiers: alphanumeric codes that help to further describe a procedure without changing the initial code itself

Coding: the process of translating a physician's documentation regarding health services into alphanumeric medical codes that are then inserted into a claim for processing

Co-insurance: the percent the patient pays for covered services as opposed to the amount the carrier pays

Comprehensive plan: commercial plan; composite of both basic and major medical coverage

Coordination of benefits: insurance policy provision stating that when a patient is covered by more than one group plan, the total benefits paid by all policies are limited to 100 percent of the charges

Co-payment: the balance of payment for covered services paid by the patient after the insurer pays its portion

Cost contract: contract between an HMO and Medicare specifying that the HMO's Medicare patients receive all care from that particular HMO

Cost plan: a point-of-service type of managed care plan in which a patient is allowed to go to outside providers and Medicare will pay its share of the cost

Coverage verification: *see* Predetermination

Cross-over contract: a type of Medigap contract in which Medicare automatically forwards claims to the Medigap carrier

Cross-over patient: one who has Medicare as his primary coverage and Medicaid as a supplemental

Current Procedural Terminology (CPT): refers to a system of coding services, procedures, and supplies developed by the American Medical Association

Customary fee: fee basis determined by insurers based on 90 percent of fees charged by all doctors in the same specialty in the same geographic area

Day sheet: page used by provider to list all daily superbill information on a single sheet rather than send one superbill per patient to the outsource biller

Deductible: the amount the patient must pay before the insurance coverage begins to kick in

Dependent: spouse, child, or other person for whom the insured is legally responsible

Drop claim to paper: a service in which a clearinghouse prints and mails a paper version of a claim received online

Dual coverage: a term meaning a patient is covered by two or more insurance policies

Durable medical equipment: walkers, wheelchairs, hospital beds, and other equipment used in and around the home because of medical necessity

Elective procedure: a medical procedure not requiring immediate action

Electronic claim: a medical claim sent electronically to an insurance carrier or clearinghouse

Electronic Data Interchange (EDI): sends information electronically from one computer to another

Electronic health record (EHR): a medical record that is maintained in an electronic (digital) format; also referred to as electronic medical record (EMR)

Enrollee: *see* Insured

Epoetin: used in the treatment of home dialysis patients

ESRD: end-stage renal disease, a kidney malfunction

Essential health benefits: health insurance plans must offer ten benefit categories including hospitalization, emergency services, maternity, and prescriptions (find a complete list at: www.healthcare.gov/glossary/essential-health-benefits/)

Evaluation and Management (E&M): the portion of the CPT codes used to categorize physician visits

Exclusions: services or problems not covered by the insurance carrier

Exclusive Provider Organization (EPO): a type of managed care organization

Explanation of Benefits (EOB): the carrier uses this to summarize the details of a submitted claim and its reimbursement

Fee-for-service plan: commercial plan in which subscribers make monthly payments that entitle them to coverage

Full-practice management: the practice of handling all aspects of a doctor's accounting as opposed to strictly processing claims

GP: general practitioner

Grandfathered health plan: a group or individual health plan created on or before March 23, 2010; exempt from many of the changes implemented by the Affordable Care Act

Gross income: the amount of income before expenses are deducted

Group policy: commercial policy written for and purchased by groups or employers for their members or employees

HCFA Common Procedure Coding System (HCPCS): the CPT coding system devised by the American Medical Association

HCFA 1500: form on which all medical insurance claims must be sent, which has been updated and is now called the CMS 1500

Health Care Financing Administration (HCFA): this is now known as the Centers for Medicare and Medicaid Services (CMS); *see* Centers for Medicare and Medicaid Service

Health Maintenance Organization (HMO): a managed care type of provider service in which patients pay a monthly fee to belong

Health Insurance Portability and Accountability Act of 1996 (HIPAA): this is designed to protect patient privacy by protecting personal health information

Indemnify: to reimburse health expenses

Indemnity policy: a policy in which the carrier reimburses the patient for covered services up to a limit set in the policy

Independent Practice Association (IPA): a type of managed care organization

Individual/family deductible: under some policies, each covered family member must meet a deductible; under other policies, all of the family's medical expenses go toward meeting one deductible

Individual policy: commercial policy written for and purchased by an individual or an individual and his family as opposed to a group policy

Insured: the policy holder; the person covered by the policy, who, because he's covered (as in a group policy), makes it possible for his family to be covered; also known as the enrollee, certificate holder, or subscriber

Insurer: the insurance company that writes and administers the insurance policy; also known as the carrier, underwriter, or administrator

International Classification of Diseases (ICD-10): a system of coding diseases developed by the World Health Organization; also called ICD-10-CM for Clinical Modification.

Intermediaries: commercial carriers that handle Medicare claims.

Level II: branch of the HCPCS coding system relating to durable medical equipment, medical supplies, and chemotherapy, among other miscellaneous services

Level III: HCPCS codes used on a local level by Medicare

Lifetime maximum: the total amount the policy will pay for a certain condition or problem for elective or non-essential health benefits

Limiting charge: the amount providers who do not accept assignment can charge over and above the Medicare-approved amount

Listed exclusions: specific services, procedures, or supplies not covered by the policy and therefore not paid by the insurance company, but can be useful if you want some added protection for your personal assets

Lock-in requirements: *see* Cost contract

Major medical plan: commercial plan designed for catastrophic situations such as extended hospitalization; does not pay for minor health problems or office visits and usually features large deductible and co-payments

Managed Service Organization (MSO): a type of managed care organization

Maximums: the top or maximum amounts a policy will pay

Medicaid: insurance program administered by CMS and each state's government for people at or near poverty level

Medicare: insurance coverage for those over age 65, younger people suffering from end-stage renal disease, and those who have been collecting Social Security disability benefits for more than two years

Medigap: supplemental Medicare coverage

Minimum premium plan (MPP): group self-insured program in which the employer provides funds for claims up to a certain dollar amount and then pays a commercial carrier to take on the remaining risk

Neurology: medical specialty dealing with the nervous system and its diseases

Nonduplication of benefits: *see* Coordination of benefits

Non-PAR: a provider who declines to accept Medicare assignment

Oncology: medical specialty concerned with tumors

Out-of-network provider: a provider who is not contracted with the health insurance plan

Outsource billing service: one that performs its work outside the provider's office

Part A Medicare: covers inpatient hospitalization, skilled nursing, and hospice and home health-care services

Part B Medicare: covers doctors' services, outpatient hospital care, X-rays, lab tests, ambulance services, durable medical equipment, and other nonhospitalization services

Participating physician (PAR): a provider who accepts Medicare assignment; also called a PAR

Pneumococcal: organism responsible for infections including pneumonia, bronchitis, and meningitis

Podiatrist: foot disorder specialist

Point-of-service plan (POS): a managed care plan; *see* Cost plan

Preauthorization: term used when the insurance carrier requires the provider to receive permission before performing a service

Predetermination: term used when the doctor determines the maximum amount he will pay for certain services, procedures, and supplies before performing or providing them; also called coverage or benefits verification

Pre-existing condition: a disease, medical condition, or problem the patient already has before he applies for insurance or before the policy takes effect

Preferred Provider Organization (PPO): a managed care organization in which a group of doctors cooperates with an insurance plan by accepting fee-for-service payments at less than the usual and customary rate

Primary physician: in an HMO-type plan, this is the patient's preassigned physician

Provider: anyone who provides health-care services and/or supplies, e.g., ambulance service, biofeedback technician, dentist, durable equipment purveyor, pharmacist, or social worker, in addition to all types of medical doctors

Psychoneurotic: refers to a type of mental illness that is not as severe as a psychosis or character disorder; neurosis

Reasonable fee: fee rate determined by insurers based on the least of: a) the fee the doctor has billed, b) the usual fee, c) the customary fee, or d) another specially justifiable fee

Reassignment: to assign payment to a third party

Referral: when one provider recommends another provider to a patient for specialized treatment or health services

Resource-based relative value scale (RBRVS): resource-based relative value scale arrives at a reasonable charge based on: a) the actual amount of work performed by the doctor;

b) the doctor's expenses, excluding malpractice insurance; and c) the cost of malpractice insurance.

Secondary claim: one in which two members of a family are supplementally covered by each other's insurance policies

Self-insured plan: type of group insurance in which the employer rather than an insurance company provides the funds to pay its employees' claims

Sender log: *see* Audit/error report

Stop-loss provision: limits the total co-payments the beneficiary must pay in a given year

Subscriber: *see* Insured

Superbill: also called a charge slip; lists the services and procedures commonly performed by the provider and gives the patient's name, date of visit, and any charges

Third-Party Administrator (TPA): an insurance or specialized management company that administers a group self-insured plan

TRICARE: provides civilian health benefits for military personnel, retirees, and dependents

UB92: form used to bill Part A Medicare

Underwriter: the insurance company that writes and administers the insurance policy; also known as the insurer, carrier, or administrator

Urologist: physician specializing in diseases of the urinary tract in both sexes and of the genital tract in the male

Usual, customary, and reasonable (UCR): method of regulating health-care costs in which insurers pay providers according to one of three schedules, the usual fee, the customary fee, or the reasonable fee

Usual fee: the usual or normal amount doctors charge for a specific service as determined by insurers who keep annual tabs and then compute an average fee

WHO: World Health Organization

Workers' compensation: provides private insurance coverage for workers who become ill or injured while on the job

Index